HITTING BACK

COMBATTING DOMESTIC VIOLENCE IN THE CRIMINAL JUSTICE SYSTEM

Matthew B. Welde, Esq.

Hitting Back

DEDICATION

A special thank you to everyone who stood by us during the hard times.

Hitting Back

ACKNOWLEDGMENTS

Pontotoc County District Attorney's Office
Chris L. Ross
Christy Wilson
Jennifer Foster
Hon. C. Steven Kessinger
Hon. Gregory D. Pollard
Hon. Lori L. Jackson
Ada Police Department
Pontotoc County Sheriff's Office
Burt Page
Family Crisis Center
Chickasaw Nation Department of Safe and Stable Families
Probation Enforcement of Oklahoma
Spokane County Prosecutor's Office
Andrea Duggan
Annette Ingham
Joseph Edwards
Ginger Johnson
Patty Wheeler
Chauntelle Lieske
Cassandra Klakken
Megan Lorincz
Safe Passage
Spokane Police Department
Spokane County Sheriff's Office
Airway Heights Police Department
Cheney Police Department
Jordan Ferguson
Erin Johnson
Kootenai County Prosecuting Attorney's Office
Stan Mortensen
Art Verharen
Laura McClinton
Julia Schoffstall

Molly Nivison
Nancy Lee
Ellie Creighton
Jodi Marhoefer

TABLE OF CONTENTS

Hitting Back

INTRODUCTION

D omestic violence is everywhere. It is a serious problem in the United States. It is a serious problem in Oklahoma. It is a serious problem in Pontotoc County. There is where I worked as a domestic violence prosecutor. I started in September 2010 and held that position until July 2016. From June of 2018 through February of 2023, I worked in Washington. I began working in Idaho in February of 2023. During my career, it was my responsibility to combat domestic violence in the criminal justice system.

Two concerns became clear to me after I took the job. One was that the domestic violence problem was too big for one person, or one agency, to deal with. I suppose we have all heard the expression *it takes a village to raise a child.* Accordingly, it also takes a village to combat domestic violence.

The reason it takes a village is that there are several fronts: Investigation, prosecution, post-conviction supervision, community outreach, community awareness, and availability of victim services. Successfully combating domestic violence is not possible unless you are combating it on all fronts.

Each front is handled by multiple agencies. These include law enforcement, courts, prosecutors, probation supervising authorities, victim service providers, and any local coordinated community response organizations.

In my experience, prosecutors are uniquely positioned to work with all the agencies involved. The prosecutor is the hub of the wagon wheel; the other agencies are the spokes. I used my position as the hub to help create and maintain the coalition of agencies necessary to combat domestic violence in Pontotoc County.

A second concern was the problem of domestic violence victims often not cooperating. Victims of most other types of crime typically cooperate.

For example, people will usually cooperate with law enforcement and prosecutors to apprehend and prosecute the person who broke into their house or stole their car.

With domestic violence cases, victim cooperation is more the exception than the rule. Thus, successfully combatting domestic violence in the criminal justice system means overcoming uncooperative victims. This is the challenge that the coalition endeavors to overcome. This book breaks those efforts down into five steps and, with the use of case examples, explains how we did it.

The first three chapters discuss my experiences as a prosecutor. This includes how I learned to do the job, the unique challenges presented by domestic violence cases, and how to overcome them. I also include examples from specific cases I prosecuted.[1]

Chapter Four addresses whether domestic violence victims should be compelled to appear in court.

Chapter Five is about the roles other agencies play. It is my hope that this book will serve as a resource for other prosecutors, law enforcement personnel, anyone else that works in any other domestic violence field, and anyone who wants to learn more about domestic violence.

This book does not refer to homicide and contains minimal discussion of sexual assault. While such crimes can certainly constitute domestic violence, the material presented here relates primarily to cases of physical abuse.

Hitting Back

4

CHAPTER ONE

Have Knowledge on Your Side

Every state in the Union has its own, often unique, statutes for crimes, punishments, evidence, and criminal procedure. Some of those statutes apply to domestic violence.

For effective prosecution, it is critical to understand all statutes that affect a domestic violence case. This includes understanding all the applicable elements for each offense. These principles are typically broken down within criminal statutes and include things like specific behaviors constituting the crime or the requisite intent.

Laws related to domestic violence offenses in Oklahoma include:

- Domestic Assault and Battery
- Domestic Assault and Battery in Presence of a Minor
- Domestic Assault and Battery with a Dangerous Weapon
- Domestic Assault and Battery against a Pregnant Woman
- Domestic Assault and Battery Resulting in Great Bodily Injury
- Domestic Assault and Battery by Strangulation

- Domestic Assault and Battery with Prior Pattern of Physical Abuse[2]

In Washington, crimes are designated as domestic violence offenses by application of a domestic violence enhancement to standard crimes where a qualifying relationship exists between the perpetrator and victim.[3]

Laws related to domestic violence offenses in Idaho include:

- Domestic Assault or Battery
- Domestic Battery with Traumatic Injury
- Domestic Assault or Battery in the Presence of a Child[4]
- Attempted Strangulation[5]

Certain domestic violence offenses are felonies while others are misdemeanors. When charging, it is important to understand the criteria needed to support a felony charge instead of a misdemeanor charge.

For example, in Oklahoma, certain charges, including Domestic Assault and Battery by Strangulation, Domestic Assault and Battery Resulting in Great Bodily Injury, or Domestic Assault and Battery with a Dangerous Weapon are felony charges on a first offense. Other charges are misdemeanors on a first offense. These same charges can be a felony if the defendant has an eligible prior conviction for domestic violence. These include Domestic Assault and Battery or Domestic Assault and Battery in Presence of Minor.[6]

In Washington, deciding the nature of a domestic violence charge is first determined by whether the standard crime is a misdemeanor or a felony. Certain standard misdemeanors can be enhanced to felonies by attaching the domestic violence designation. These include charges of assault fourth degree, violation of an order such as a protection order, harassment, and stalking.[7]

In Idaho, domestic battery is a felony if it resulted in a traumatic injury such as an external or internal wound, whether of a minor or serious nature, caused by physical force.[8] Like Oklahoma, an instance of domestic battery in Idaho can also be a felony if the defendant has prior domestic violence convictions.[9] Attempted strangulation is also a felony in Idaho.[10]

Prosecutors should understand the sentencing options and requirements for domestic violence offenses in your state or jurisdiction. This includes understanding the rules of evidence (especially regarding character evidence and self-defense) and understanding criminal procedure (especially with regards to bond and release conditions).

Effectively prosecuting domestic violence does not end with a good understanding of statutes. It is also important to have knowledge of pertinent case law. This is critical because many legal standards and principles are based on prior court decisions. A prosecutor often relies on case law for issues such as whether a defendant has met the threshold to assert the defense of self-defense, admissibility of recorded 911 calls, admissibility of recorded jail phone calls, admissibility of body worn camera videos, admissibility of a defendant's statements, whether an out-of-court statement is inadmissible hearsay or testimonial.

Effective prosecution also requires an understanding of domestic violence and the dynamics of abusive relationships. This means understanding both batterer and victim behavior. For batterer behavior, a prosecutor should understand the cycle of violence and the power and control wheel.[11]

A domestic violence prosecutor should also understand how batterers create common circumstances such as isolation and dependence and how those circumstances affect victims. This includes knowing how fear is a strong factor affecting victim behavior and how victims are affected by trauma.

Some of this knowledge can be obtained through formal training such as seminars or conferences. Some can be obtained by working with more experienced domestic violence prosecutors.

Finally, as a domestic violence prosecutor, having proficient expertise extends beyond your personal knowledge. As mentioned in the introduction, it takes a village. It is important to have other people's knowledge on your side as well.

You Don't Get to Choose Your Victim

An important step in having knowledge on your side is participating in formal training. Most law schools do not offer classes on domestic violence prosecution and not everyone can intern in the domestic violence unit at the nearest District Attorney, County Attorney, Prosecuting Attorney, or State Attorney's Office. So, for a lot of beginning prosecutors, that means holding the position before you are up to speed on how to effectively prosecute domestic violence cases.

In May of 2011 I attended a two-day conference called *The Prosecutor Bootcamp,* which is an annual conference for new prosecutors offered by the Oklahoma District Attorney's Council.

The Prosecutor Bootcamp was not a domestic violence conference. It focused on material with general applicability such as case evaluation, enhancement statutes[12], the Oklahoma Uniform Jury Instructions[13], and victim's rights; however, I still acquired some helpful knowledge that started me on the path to being an effective prosecutor.

One section of the bootcamp that was helpful regarding domestic violence was the section on case evaluation. This is the process by which a prosecutor decides whether more evidence is needed, evaluates the strength of the evidence already collected, decides whether to file any charges, decides what charges to file[14], assesses the availability and reliability of witnesses, and reviews the defendant's criminal history.

Another important facet of handling domestic violence cases is the need to evaluate the victim. This should include the victim's credibility by checking to see if the victim has any criminal history, outstanding warrants, pending criminal charges, etc.

It is also essential to know if the victim has any substance abuse issues. Victims that have a troubled past, addiction issues, or a criminal record are still victims. They do not deserve to be abused, and such cases must be prosecuted; however, background problems, especially if initially unrecognized, can be a major obstacle in court. Some of these issues can be topics for cross examination when the victim is testifying. Jurors will evaluate a victim's credibility just like they evaluate credibility for any other witness.

There are other items a prosecutor needs to consider. One of these is ascertaining whether the victim is cooperative. Often that is not the case. This can be a fluid situation because, in some situations, the victim will initially cooperate only to become uncooperative later. When this occurs, it's important to ascertain whether the victim is still in the relationship with the batterer.

Another concern is knowing whether the victim can be located. A victim who does not want to be served with a subpoena can sometimes be very difficult to find.

Additionally, an issue is ascertaining whether the victim has a history of making domestic abuse allegations. Such a fact, if true, does not mean the current allegations are false. Nonetheless, this is information a prosecutor needs to know. I learned this last one the hard way.

In January 2012, I was in court for a preliminary hearing for a defendant charged with Domestic Assault and Battery by Strangulation.[15]

The victim was on the witness stand at the preliminary hearing and the defense attorney was conducting his cross examination. One line of questioning was about whether the police had ever previously been called out to the victim's residence for a domestic violence situation. The victim testified that she had not previously been involved in any domestic altercations where law enforcement was called.

That was a lie. I did not know that she was lying, but the defense attorney knew it. The defense attorney had a stack of police reports sitting in front of him from instances where the police had been previously called out to the victim's residence for domestic violence situations.

I should have known about those previous situations just like the defense attorney did. That case ended up getting dismissed, and I learned a valuable lesson about not having the knowledge on my side.

Portland is Nice This Time of Year

In January 2013, I attended a four-day domestic violence training conference in Portland Oregon. While there, I mingled with prosecutors learning about the challenges involved in prosecuting domestic violence cases. The knowledge I obtained at that conference was tremendous. I was presented with ideas that had never even occurred to me, and I had questions answered that I did not know I needed to ask. The knowledge I obtained at that conference not only made me a better prosecutor, but also gave me the skills to educate and train other people, such as law enforcement officers.

One lesson I learned at the conference pertained to strangulation. As I mentioned earlier, it's important to understand all the elements for each domestic violence offense. For a defendant charged with Domestic Assault and Battery by Strangulation, one of the elements is asphyxiation.[16] Understanding what asphyxiation is and proving that it happened are two different things.[17] In some cases, there may be identifiable ligature marks or bruising on the victim's neck. Often, however, no such marks or bruising are present.

Asphyxiation does not require as much pressure as bruising because it doesn't take much pressure to cut off the blood flow to the brain.[18] In cases lacking marks or bruising, proving asphyxiation can be difficult. Even a cooperative victim testifying to the strangulation will not constitute proof beyond a reasonable doubt. The prosecutor's case will be stronger if the claim can be corroborated.

One way to corroborate a strangulation claim is by proving any other allegations the victim made about the incident. Consider a hypothetical case where the victim claimed she was struck in the eye with a closed fist, pushed against the wall, and then choked.[19]

If there is a photograph of the victim's face showing a black eye and there is damage to the wall where the victim claimed she was pushed, then two out of the three details are corroborated.

This allows the prosecutor to argue that the victim's claim that she was strangled should also be believed. This still may not be evidence beyond a reasonable doubt. There are other types of physical evidence that show evidence of strangulation.

One example is petechial hemorrhaging on the victim's eyelids, periorbital areas of the eyes, lower lip, or hair line. Other examples include contusions behind the ears, diffi-culty swallowing, and voice changes. Difficulty swallowing and voice changes are referred to as non-visible symptoms.

Third-party witness testimony can be supportive, but batterers rarely strangle their victims in the presence of others.

Another evidentiary sign of strangulation is scratch marks. When this topic was presented, my first thought was about scratch marks left by the batterer. In my experience, I rarely saw strangulation cases where the batterer left scratch marks on the victim. So, my first thought was "What good is that?"

I learned the topic of scratch marks is not about the batterer, it's about the victim. If you want direct evidence to corroborate a victim's strangulation claim, look for vertical scratches at the base of the jaw line or around the clavicles.

In the past, I've seen scratches fitting that description, but I had never connected them to strangulation. Instead, I viewed those scratches in the same way I viewed a black eye or a swollen lip. I simply considered these as injuries the victim sustained during the assault.

I now know such vertical scratch marks are likely self-inflicted wounds resulting from the victim's efforts to pry the batterer's hands or arm away from her throat or neck.

That piece of knowledge made so much sense that I wondered how I had failed to realize it. After the conference, I was armed with something tangible to look for in the absence of bruising or ligature marks. This was also a valuable piece of knowledge to pass on to law enforcement personnel. I made sure to share it after I returned home. Law enforcement personnel in the field are more effective when they're better informed about what to look for.

Another valuable piece of knowledge I brought home from the Portland conference pertained to recorded jail phone calls.

I had been aware that domestic violence victims often sought to drop the charges against their batterer. It was such a common occurrence that, in Oklahoma, our staff kept a legal pad handy at the reception window for victims to write out their requests. Those written requests became known as yellow pad letters. I often had these waiting for me on Monday mornings.

Prior to the Portland conference, I was aware that the Pontotoc County jail had an inmate phone system that recorded the inmate phone calls. I had obtained copies of recorded phone calls from the Sherriff's Office for use in other types of cases, but I had not used recorded jail calls as a tool for prosecuting domestic violence.

I also learned the connection between recorded jail calls and yellow pad letters. Prior to the Portland conference, it had never occurred to me that a primary reason I was receiving yellow pad letters was because batterers were calling their victims from the jail and "encouraging" them to have the charges dropped.

Once I started listening to the phone calls, I learned that "encouragement" came in several forms. Batterers would sometimes try to inflame and then exploit their victim's feelings of guilt by saying things like "You don't want me to go to jail, do you?" In other instances, batterers would try a victim blaming approach by saying things like "Why did you do this to me?"

Batterers would sometimes make explicit or implicit threats such as pointing out that they will lose their job if the charges do not get dropped (implying that financial hardship would result for the victim) or that they will end the relationship if the charges are not dropped.

Statements like these are examples of why a good understanding of batterer behavior, the power and control wheel, and the cycle of violence are important. Victims trapped in abusive relationships who have been isolated and who are dependent on the batterer are susceptible to this "encouragement." In more extreme instances, batterers would make threats of additional physical harm. In my experience though, it's rare for batterers to make explicit threats of additional physical harm on recorded jail calls.

Upon my return from Portland, I adopted a new approach with regards to yellow pad letters. The first thing I did was work with our staff to make sure that any domestic violence victim submitting a yellow pad letter included a phone number. Obtaining a current phone number is important for contacting them to discuss the case.

Obtaining victim phone numbers serves a second purpose. They provide a means to search for recorded jail calls. Searching by phone number is the most efficient method for obtaining recordings of calls to victims.

My new approach was to request jail calls made to the victim's phone number every time I received a yellow pad letter in a case where the defendant was contesting his charges and had served any significant jail time.[20]

The results of increased screening of inmate phone calls were astounding. Many of the jail call requests I submitted resulted in useful recordings that contained statements usable in court as evidence against the batterer, including statements that "encouraged" the victims to drop the charges.

Additional examples of communication issues are discussed later in the book.

Another one of the conference sessions included an in-depth study of the doctrine of *forfeiture by wrongdoing*, which included the burden of proof and relevant case law.[21] I was previously aware of the doctrine, but I had not researched it or tried to use it.

Forfeiture by wrongdoing allows for admission of statements against the defendant that would otherwise be inadmissible as hearsay or as a violation of the defendant's right to confrontation where the defendant wrongfully caused, or acquiesced in wrongfully causing, that witness' unavailability with the intent to prevent that witness from testifying or cooperating with a criminal prosecution. That is quite a mouth full. To put it more simply, if a defendant intentionally prevents a witness from testifying or cooperating, then that defendant cannot prevent prior statements by that witness from being admitted because the defendant has forfeited his objection. When paired with statements found in recorded inmate jail calls, this doctrine can be extremely powerful.

When a prosecutor is faced with a victim that cannot be located or fails to appear to testify, then a search for jail calls between the defendant and that victim should follow. The recordings might include statements by the defendant that will support a forfeiture by wrongdoing action.

Another topic covered at the Portland conference provided me with valuable knowledge pertained to working with victims of domestic violence. These victims often recant or choose not to cooperate with the prosecution, which can be difficult and frustrating. Thus, prosecutors are often tasked with overcoming this hurdle while trying to hold the batterer accountable.

Prior to my trip to Portland, one approach I used to overcome uncooperative victims was to tell victims that their cooperation would reduce the likelihood that their children would need to testify in court. This approach was only available in cases where children were present during the assault, but such circumstances were common.[22] During the conference, I learned why that was not a good approach.

Part of textbook batterer behavior is to manipulate their victims to maintain the abusive relationship. I found that my approach was doing the same thing. I was manipulating the victim to maintain my case. After I returned home from Portland, I never used that approach again. Ever. Sometimes having the knowledge on your side means knowing what not to do.

Right Around the Bend

In August 2016, I attended the Oregon District Attorney's Office Annual Summer Conference. This was a three-day event held in Bend, Oregon.

The first day consisted of four sessions on training for domestic violence prosecutors. The first two sessions were about the neurobiology of domestic and sexual violence. The second two covered trauma literacy and interview techniques.

Neurobiology is about what is happening inside the brains of domestic and sexual violence victims. This includes discussions on what trauma means, how trauma affects brain function, how the brain recognizes and responds to threatening situations, and the specific areas in the brain that are involved or affected.

This includes how the prefrontal cortex is impaired during an assault and how that injury means that the victim is only able to use reflex and habitual behavior. We learned about how attachment networks in the brain inhibit threat networks, thereby causing confusion. Victims of repeated trauma can end up with a fear based neural network that impairs the prefrontal cortex and impairs the victim's ability to differentiate.

An example of a victim losing the ability to differentiate is where the facial expression a batterer makes when upset about anything equates to the face he makes when upset at the victim. The result is fear of another assault.

The second neurobiology topic introduced the concept of tonic immobility. This is a form of paralysis that can occur after a failed struggle. It includes collapsed immobility, which can be brought on by extreme fear and anxiety when there is no perceived escape.

Threat circuitry in a person's brain can take over in a traumatic experience. This causes an involuntary focus on survival and coping. This involuntary focus makes it less likely that the victim will notice details that are not part of survival or coping. This leads to peripheral details being vulnerable to change because fewer peripheral details get encoded and consolidated during a traumatic event.

A related topic was about how an impaired Broca's Area, which is a part of the brain, can affect the victim's capacity to talk about what happened. This includes the victim having difficulty finding the correct words to describe what happened, or even being willing to participate in an interview.

All the material in these sessions was helpful with regards to understanding why victims behave the way they do during interviews or while testifying and how to work through it.

Trying to work with uncooperative domestic violence or sexual assault victims, or victims that have difficulty remembering, is less frustrating if you understand why they are not cooperating or are having trouble remembering.

The afternoon sessions taught how to apply the neurobiology material from the morning sessions. A sound understanding of what is going on inside the victim's head is important as the case moves through the criminal justice process.

The core component of the afternoon sessions was FETI. That stands for Forensic Experiential Trauma Interview. FETI is a method of interviewing victims that considers how trauma affects the brain.

The first step in FETI is genuine empathy. This is important for any domestic violence prosecutor or any law enforcement investigator to remember, because working with domestic violence or sexual assault victims can be frustrating. A key aspect of FETI is that it is a nonconfrontational approach. The presenters analogized this by using the terms "soft eyes" versus "hard eyes" with regards to tone, demeanor, and body language being non-confrontational instead of confrontational.

After learning about FETI, I compared it to my existing approach. I found a lot of symmetry because it was already my approach to be non-confrontational. I also found one significant divergence between my existing approach and FETI. The divergence was the form of the questions I asked.

My approach involved asking direct questions about the facts of the incident and about specific details with standard who, what, when, where, why, and how questions. These are confrontational questions. The form of these questions fails to consider how trauma affects a victim's behavior and ability to remember or explain a traumatic experience.

After the conference, I changed my approach to better incorporate FETI techniques. That meant trading out my confrontational questions focused on the incident in favor of more open questions that offered the victim the opportunity to tell me about the experience and the feelings involved. A trauma victim's responses would often be disjointed and fragmented but would eventually include enough fragments to create a complete picture of what happened. I now understand that there is a more effective way to interview a domestic or sexual assault victim. It is just one more piece of knowledge that I have on my side.

The Nurse Spends More Time with the Patient

In early November, 2019, I attended a training event called Identifying and Investigating Asphyxiation, Strangulation, Suffocation, and Aquatic Crimes. The seminar was held in Spokane at the Washington State University Riverpoint Campus. Two new ideas came out of that training event that improved my ability to prosecute strangulation cases. Strangulation is a common occurrence in abusive relationships. Thus, having the tools to effectively prosecute it is important.

The first topic was that proving strangulation is more about non-visible effects than visible marks. The second was the introduction of using strangulation experts at trial.

Previously, my evaluation of strangulation cases placed more emphasis on visible marks, such as ligature marks, red marks, or bruising, on or near the victim's neck. At this training event, I learned that it can be more effective to prove strangulation by focusing on the non-visible effects. The function of a strangulation expert is to explain in detail the non-visible effects to a jury and how easy it is to strangle a victim.

There is a wide array of potential non-visible effects of strangulation. These include intuitive effects like sore throat, dizziness, or neck pain. The victim may have also experienced less intuitive effects like numbness or tingling in the extremities and headaches.

At trial, a strangulation expert, focusing on both visible and non-visible effects, presents a stronger case than merely relying on visible marks. The non-visible effects get the most focus, with the approach culminating in an argument that the victim would not know to report the non-visible effects unless the victim experienced them. Post-trial discussions with jurors from strangulation trials have confirmed that this approach is effective.

The strangulation experts I have worked with have always been Sexual Assault Nurse Examiners (SANE nurses). That is because SANE nurses receive strangulation training. One common approach defense attorneys use is to ask the nurse if they are a doctor. That question is meant to attack the nurse's credibility. Our response is to ask the expert whether the nurse or doctor spends more time with the patient. Post-trial discussions with jurors have confirmed that this approach is effective.

The Only Way to Learn It is to Do It

Another important step in having the knowledge on your side is to learn from more experienced prosecutors. This includes asking questions and observing them during court proceedings.

Doing this can only get you so far, however. At some point, you must walk into the courtroom and handle matters yourself. A pair of misdemeanor domestic violence trials from early in my career help illustrate this point.

The first was a misdemeanor bench trial with which my boss helped.[23] A bench trial is a trial without a jury where the judge decides whether the defendant is guilty or not guilty.

My boss put on the trial, and I watched. At the trial, the victim recanted her original claim of abuse. Fortunately, the victim's original claims had been preserved in the written statement she gave to law enforcement.

I had an opportunity to observe an experienced prosecutor confront a recanting victim with her own written statement. He did so flawlessly. The trial resulted in a guilty verdict.

The second was a misdemeanor bench trial that took place just five days later. I handled the second trial myself.[24] Like the previous trial, the victim recanted her original claim of abuse and was confronted with her original statement.

Unlike the previous trial, there was an acquittal. I did not properly confront the victim with her testimony before impeaching her with her original statement. Ultimately, there was not enough corroborating evidence to prove the victim's original claim beyond a reasonable doubt. I learned from that experience and was much more prepared to handle similar situations in the future.

Our work with strangulation experts in Washington is another example of learning through practice. For the first trial where a strangulation expert testified, I had a script of questions taken from the drawing board. After each trial, I met with jurors to receive feedback regarding the strangulation expert. Over time, and with the help of feedback from more and more jurors, my list of questions greatly improved.

In the earlier references to yellow pad letters and recorded jail calls, I mentioned the importance of obtaining a phone number for contacting victims to discuss the case. With uncooperative victims, this is especially important.

Domestic violence prosecutors should meet with uncooperative victims face-to-face. This is another area where a prosecutor must learn through practice. There are several reasons why this is important.

First, every victim is unique, and learning to work with them effectively is an important part of successful prosecution.

Second, face-to-face meetings are the best way to build rapport with the victim and answer their questions. Direct contact also helps clear up any misconceptions the victim may have and might reveal why the victim does not want to cooperate with the prosecution.

It is not always necessary to meet with an uncooperative victim. In misdemeanor first offense domestic violence cases in Oklahoma, it was common for the defendant to enter a plea of guilty or no contest. Otherwise, meeting with the victim was essential. Not every uncooperative victim provides a yellow pad letter or reaches out to the prosecutor, which can make them difficult to get a hold of. Others will decline the offer to meet in person.

In Washington, misdemeanor domestic violence cases rarely resolved as quickly.[25] But it remained true that uncooperative victims often did not contact the prosecutor, respond to the prosecutor's attempts to make contact, or provide law enforcement with correct contact information.

Depending on time constraints on the prosecutor's case-load, it may be necessary to prioritize which victims to meet with in person. These criteria should include giving priority to felonies over misdemeanors, and the likelihood that the victim may need to testify.

For victim meetings, knowledge of domestic violence, the dynamics of abusive relationships, batterer behavior, victim behavior, and trauma-informed interview techniques is critical. A lack of such knowledge will likely result in the prosecutor asking the wrong questions, failing to ask the right questions, and neglecting to discuss important topics. There are several steps that a prosecutor should take when meeting with an uncooperative victim.

The first step is scheduling a closed-door meeting with a female third-party witness present. The victim should be encouraged to openly and honestly discuss issues related to the case. Assuring the victim that the meeting is private will typically help her feel comfortable and encourage full participation. It is important, however, to qualify the privacy of the meeting. The victim should be informed that some statements, particularly those about the facts of the case, may need to be shared with the defense attorney. Having a third-party witness present is important for this reason, and for other reasons as well.

Ideally, the third-party witness should be a victim advocate. When an in-house advocate or victim/witness coordinator is available, that person is the best choice. If an in-house victim/witness coordinator or advocate is not available, then arranging for an advocate from a local victim services provider might also work.

If there is no outside victim advocate available, then whatever alternative the prosecutor goes with needs to be a female. Having another woman in the room will likely help the victim feel more comfortable.[26]

It appears I am assuming the victim will be a woman. In some cases, batterers are women and victims are men. I treated cases with female batterers the same as cases with male batterers. After many years as a domestic violence prosecutor, I could probably count on two hands the number of victim meetings I had with male victims.

In addition to helping the victim feel more comfortable, the presence of a victim/witness coordinator or advocate can help the discussion because of the input they can offer. A prosecutor with an understanding of domestic violence, the dynamics of abusive relationships, batterer behavior, and victim behavior may still not be equivalent to a trained victim/witness coordinator or advocate. It's likely that the victim will have questions about victim services or other topics that the victim/witness coordinator or advocate would be more qualified to answer.

Uncooperative victims are often nervous, come into the meeting with a defensive mindset, and expect the meeting to be confrontational or adversarial. A good technique is to open each meeting with a polite greeting and a sincere thank you for coming. Offer to let the victim say anything she wants and ask any questions she wants. Then let her continue as long as she wants. This can extend the meeting beyond thirty minutes, but the time investment will be worth it in the long run.

Victims often provide a wealth of useful knowledge, and active listening is the key. The prosecutor or advocate might ask a question or two if something the victim said needs clarification, but interruptions should be kept to a minimum. First and foremost, the victim should be encouraged to explain why she didn't want to cooperate. In these instances, there is a likelihood that the victim's concerns are something that can be addressed.

For example, many victims say they do not want to cooperate because they don't want their batterer to go to jail or prison. Often that is because they want their batterer to get help with his problems and they believe he will not receive any help while incarcerated.

Another common reason is that victims do not want their batterer to lose his job. This is a signal that the victim has financial concerns or feels financially dependent on her batterer.

Understanding these concerns is important. There may be a good chance to relieve the worries of an uncooperative victim. If these concerns can be effectively addressed, an uncooperative victim may become cooperative.

Once the victim has finished sharing her concerns and asking questions, her demeanor is typically more relaxed. They often become less defensive because the meeting does not turn out to be as confrontational or adversarial as expected. This is a good time to pursue the third goal, which is to explain the details of the case.

The first detail should be to clarify that you are trying to be honest and candid. This includes letting her know you will give straight answers to all questions with no evasiveness or legal jargon.

The prosecutor should also make it clear that the victim may not like everything she is told. The prosecutor should also tell her it's okay to say if she doesn't understand or disagrees with what she hears. Showing the victim respect and consideration also serves as an effective transition to the next point.

This second point is the no-drop policy. When unco-operative victims come to the meeting, their goal is often to have the charges dropped. Throughout my time as a prosecutor, the offices where I worked maintained a no-drop policy. We would not dismiss a case at the victim's request. An explanation can be found later in this book. I explained that the Prosecutor's Office had picked up the case and decided to pursue it. The importance of this policy cannot be overstated. Prosecution of a case is not the victim's decision.

An upside of this policy is that it empowers victims to use the policy as a shield against accusations that they are the ones pressing charges. The victims can then tell their batterers, that person's family, or anyone else, that it was not up to them to drop the charges. Also, after attending the meeting, victims can tell those people that they tried to drop the charges but could not because it was not their choice.

The third point concerns explaining the facts of the case. This may not always be necessary, but, in many cases, there are factual inconsistencies or unanswered questions that can be addressed during victim meetings. I do not turn these meetings into full interviews like an investigator might do.

When necessary, I address what happened to the victims and ask questions. When this happens, it is important to document the victim's responses because their statements will need to be disclosed to the defense.

The fourth point involves explaining what the specific charge or charges are, any plea recommendations, and where the case is in the criminal justice process.

Discussing the plea recommendation can be complicated. Typically, these are discussed with the victim before being presented to the batterer and his attorney. There are two reasons for this policy.

First, victims, even if uncooperative, should be consulted regarding a plea recommendation before it is extended. In most states, perhaps all states, there is a victim's rights statute or a list of victim's rights requiring that a victim be informed and/or consulted regarding plea negotiations. This is not possible if, in rare cases, a recommendation or plea offer is extended before talking with the victim.

A good technique when discussing plea recommendations with the victims is comparing the process to a pie chart. Do this by explaining that the victim's input is the big piece of the pie. Also note, though, that other issues are pieces of the pie that must be considered. These include the seriousness of the incident, the batterer's criminal history, or how similar cases have been handled in the past.

Another reason to discuss the plea recommendation with the victim before extending it is to address any concerns she may have shared earlier. This is important when deciding whether probation or incarceration will be recommended. Incarceration is an issue where the victim should have the most influence. If a victim wants the charges dropped, she will be unlikely to support incarceration, and the victim's preference is still influential because an uncooperative victim is still a victim.

A victim's input regarding probation or incarceration can, and should, be influential but not final. In certain cases, where the facts and circumstances are more severe, recommending incarceration regardless of what the victim wants may be necessary. That decision should be explained to the victim.

In less severe cases, it is often a good practice to address a victim's concerns by agreeing to offer probation instead of incarceration. Any recommendation for probation would typically include counseling for domestic violence.[27] This way, two common victim concerns can be resolved since the batterer is not going to be incarcerated and will have the opportunity to receive help.

Another issue is the batterer's employment. No promise should be made to a victim that the batterer will be able to keep his job. A good technique to use here might be explaining the batterer's chances of keeping his job are far better on probation. This may be a relief for the victim if she believes he will at least have a chance to maintain gainful employment.

If the meeting is about a misdemeanor case, it is a good technique to explain that misdemeanors are typically less of a hindrance to employment than felonies, but I would qualify this by explaining that while it is typically true, there are some professions where even a misdemeanor domestic abuse charge can result in termination. It is important to not sugar coat anything.

The next point, after the plea recommendation discussion is over, concerns whether the defendant will accept the decision. He still has the right to reject the offer or recommendation and fight the case.

If he rejects it, it's necessary to ask the victim if she will support prosecution. At this point, the victim may ask if that means she would have to testify in court. The victim should be told that his rejection means she will probably have to testify. Fortunately, most victims still answer yes. This is more likely to occur if he rejects the opportunity to get help. Experience has shown that in cases where batterers reject probation offers, the victims nearly always stay true to their word.

This point was only brought up in cases where I agreed to offer probation. While uncooperative victims often agreed to cooperate if it meant the batterer received probation and counseling, they rarely agreed to cooperate in incarcerating him.

The Apple Doesn't Fall....

Uncooperative domestic violence victims are often motivated by fear. This includes worries of what will happen to them if their batterer is prosecuted. In some cases, uncooperative victims have fears that a prosecutor is either unaware of or cannot address. This is particularly true in cases where the plea recommendation and likely outcome of the case is incarceration.

With the dynamics of abusive relationships being what they are,[28] incarceration of a batterer often results in a great deal of hardship for the victim. In such cases, the victim is likely trying to get the charges dropped to avoid impending adversity.

Dilemmas the victim might be afraid of, whether they are financial or otherwise, may be amplified if there are minor children involved. It is important for a prosecutor to understand that these fears are valid, and that whatever the victim is afraid of is likely to happen.

Unfortunately, I've prosecuted cases where the victim's fears were realized. In one case, the batterer was ultimately incarcerated.[29] The assault took place on a Saturday. I became aware of it the following Monday. When I arrived that morning, the yellow pad letter was already waiting for me. I immediately scheduled a meeting with the victim.

The police officers did a good job working the scene. The body camera video was air-tight. The defendant had a lengthy criminal history, including a prior domestic violence conviction, and was on probation. It was a case where incarceration would be recommended, regardless of what the victim wanted.

When meeting with the victim, I used the approach described in the previous section. Since the batterer was not going to receive a probation recommendation, there was very little chance that the victim was going to be cooperative. As the meeting went on, she became more insistent that I drop the charges. At different points, she gave me alternate versions of what happened.

At one point, to try and explain the lump she had on her forehead when the police arrived, she insisted she fell in the bedroom and hit her head on the footboard of the bed. Later, she insisted that she fell in the kitchen and hit her head on the edge of the counter.

When I asked her whether she fell in the kitchen or bedroom, she did not budge. She was desperate and clearly motivated by fear. During the meeting, neither the advocate nor I were able to learn what hardships she was afraid of.

I later found out why she was so desperate to get the charges dropped. The batterer's father owned the house that she lived in with their children. She had no job or source of income. Additionally, she had no family or support system in the area. She was isolated and dependent on her batterer financially.

Another fear she had was if her batterer was incarcerated, his father would evict her and her children (his own grand-children) from that house. That would leave her homeless and jobless with children to care for. She was trying desper-ately to avoid such a fate.

Sadly, she was not able to avoid that fate. The apple did not fall far from the tree, and when her batterer was incar-cerated in the Oklahoma Department of Corrections, her worst fears came true. His father evicted her and her children. That case remains the quintessential example of how real and valid a domestic violence victim's fear can be. It is important for a prosecutor to understand that whatever a victim is afraid of is probably going to happen.

This is Why I Do This

In September of 2015, I participated in Partnership Confer-ence on Domestic Violence, Sexual Assault, and Stalking in Norman, Oklahoma.

I was both an attendee and a presenter. The conference's closing general session included the description of a domes-tic violence homicide case. The defendant was Tommy Castro. He was convicted of murdering a five-year-old girl.

The facts of the case were heinous. One aspect of the presentation was the investigation into his criminal history and background. That investigation revealed that he had a 20-year history of viciously abusive relationships involving numerous victims, both women and children, and that he continually managed to evade any accountability or consequences for his actions.

I'm not going to recreate that entire presentation here. Instead, I want to share what I took from it. Tommy Castro evaded prosecution and accountability because his victims were too afraid of him to cooperate, and for good reason. Tommy Castro was a monster. His background included a long string of cases with uncooperative victims, and he evaded consequences because those cases were not sufficiently investigated or prosecuted.

The Tommy Castro case reflects the importance of prosecuting all domestic violence cases, whether the victim is cooperative or not. It is important for prosecutors to obtain the knowledge and tools necessary to successfully prosecute cases without the victim's cooperation because if a prosecutor chooses to drop cases with uncooperative victims, then that prosecutor runs the risk of enabling the next Tommy Castro.

A prosecutor cannot be effective if he lacks an understanding of victim behavior, batterer behavior, the dynamics of domestic violence, the significance of certain types of evidence commonly involved, the laws pertaining to domestic violence cases, and how to deal with courtroom issues that are often a part of prosecuting them. Put simply, to be a good prosecutor, you must have knowledge on your side.

CHAPTER TWO

Have the Law on Your Side

As mentioned in Chapter One, a good understanding of statutory and case law pertaining to domestic violence is necessary to be an effective prosecutor. There are several situations or circumstances where deeper knowledge of applicable laws can positively affect the outcome of a case. If you have that understanding, then you can have the law on your side when prosecuting cases. Also, if there is a problem with the law, you may be able to change it.

You Get Only One Bite at That Apple

In most states, including the three states where I have practiced, domestic violence offenses are enhanceable. That means that people who have been convicted of domestic violence in the past may face greater potential punishment if they get convicted again.[30]

In Oklahoma, this is referred to as a "second and subsequent" offense.[31] A significant aspect of enhanced offenses is that they are felonies, whereas many first offense domestic violence cases are misdemeanors.[32] While the law allows a defendant with a prior conviction to be charged with a felony, it is not mandatory. The prosecutor has discretion on filing a misdemeanor charge instead of a felony. In one extreme example, I know of one individual who was charged and convicted for misdemeanor domestic abuse four times in a three-year period even though any of the last three cases could have been filed as felony offenses.[33]

I used a more aggressive approach in that the felony offense is called "second and subsequent" and not "third and subsequent" or "fourth and subsequent." When it came to misdemeanor domestic violence charges, my point of view was that everybody got one bite at that apple. That was it.

Most states, including the three states where I practiced, count comparable convictions from other states. Thus, an applicable prior conviction might be from another state.[34] When I received a new domestic violence case file, I thoroughly reviewed all sources of information that I had about that person's arrest record or criminal history. If I found any reference to an arrest, charge, or conviction for domestic violence I investigated those to see which of them, if any, resulted in convictions and took the necessary steps to obtain documentation to prove those convictions.[35] Cases where I found applicable prior convictions were filed as felonies. No exceptions.

The second part involved first offense misdemeanor cases, which the majority of the domestic violence cases I filed in Oklahoma fell under. Most of the time there was no enhancer to be found, and the cases lacked the circumstances necessary to file a first offense felony, such as strangulation, great bodily harm, or use of a weapon. Any plea deal I agreed to in a misdemeanor domestic violence case included making it an enhancer if that defendant were to re-offend. No exceptions. That way, if that batterer's name came across my desk again in a new domestic violence case, it would be a felony. I employed a similar approach for first-offense misdemeanor cases in Washington.

With Intent to....

Anyone who has worked as a prosecutor has likely seen that phrase many times. It can be found in the language of many criminal statutes and jury instructions. Its presence signifies that a crime is a specific intent, and its absence signifies that a crime is a general intent crime.[36] Specific intent crimes are those where the offender committed an act with the intent to achieve further intended action or consequence.[37] The distinction between specific intent crimes and general intent crimes is important. In Oklahoma, many of the domestic abuse crimes are general intent crimes.[38] In Idaho, the crime of domestic battery is also a general intent crime.[39] Conversely, other domestic abuse crimes I have prosecuted are specific intent crimes.[40]

This is important for three reasons. First, the general intent nature of most domestic violence crimes can help overcome certain arguments a defense attorney might make. Second, the general intent nature of most domestic violence crimes can help overcome cases where the victim has either recanted her original claim or tried to minimize the abuse.[41] Third, the general intent nature of most domestic violence crimes is necessary to effectively criminalize domestic abuse.

Anyone who has been a domestic violence prosecutor for even just a year or two can likely describe a case where the defense attorney's arguments included that the defendant did not injure or intend to injure the victim. In my experience such arguments are particularly likely in cases where there is little or no sign of physical injury.

Consider this hypothetical scenario. You are prosecuting a misdemeanor domestic violence case. The facts of the case are that the defendant cornered his wife in a bedroom of their home during a verbal argument and then, as the argument became more heated, grabbed her by the forearms to keep her in front of him and pushed her further into the corner. When the police responded they noticed and photographed some red areas on the victim's forearms but were not able to find or photograph any bruising, scratching, or other signs of physical injury. The case proceeds to trial. At the end of the trial the defense attorney argues that the defendant did not injure or intend to injure the victim.

For a general intent crime, it does not matter whether the victim was physically injured or whether the defendant intended to injure her. In fact, in that scenario, it is true that the defendant had no intent to cause physical injury. If the crime is a general intent, then that defendant is guilty. Any time a person does what the hypothetical husband did then that person has committed domestic abuse. If the defense attorney comes out swinging regarding intent there is no reason to back down since the law is on your side.

I will add a few additional facts to the hypothetical. During the trial, the victim testified and did not recant her original version but did try to minimize by testifying that she did not believe that the defendant was trying to injure her, that she was not injured, that the defendant had been under a lot of stress, and that she had said things to make him angry during the verbal argument. None of those claims exonerate the defendant charged with a general intent crime.

If all domestic abuse crimes were specific intent crimes, then, in that hypothetical scenario, the defendant would be not guilty. Think about that for a minute. If all domestic violence crimes were specific intent crimes, then it would be perfectly legal for someone to do what that hypothetical defendant did since there was no intent to injure. It would be hard to overstate how much harder domestic violence prosecution would be if that were the case. Certainly, if that were the case, the law would not be on your side. Obviously, that would be ridiculous, but it illustrates why it is so important that many domestic abuse crimes are general intent crimes.

Crack the Code....

In the introduction to Chapter One, I mentioned that it is critical for a prosecutor to have a good understanding of all statutes that may affect a domestic violence case. I also listed some general examples. Regardless of which state a prosecutor is working in, there will be numerous statutes to sort through. For domestic violence prosecutors that are just starting out or are early in their careers, there may be important statutes they are not aware of. That was certainly the case for me. Over the first few years of my career, I kept discovering statutes that I was previously unaware of. In this section I am going to discuss a few of these. While I'm using Oklahoma statutes to make this point, I had similar experiences when learning the statutes in Washington and Idaho; however, my experience in Oklahoma helped me learn the statutes in Washington and Idaho much faster and helped me to know what statutes to look for. Hopefully this section will help newer domestic violence prosecutors crack the code faster than I did in Oklahoma.

The first statute deals with the defendant's bond in a domestic violence case. It is likely that any experienced prosecutor has heard a defense attorney argue that the purpose of bond is to ensure the defendant's appearance at future court settings. It is not uncommon for that argument to be paired with references to the defendant's ties to the community and so forth.[42] With regards to domestic violence cases, that argument is not entirely accurate. While assuring the defendant's reappearance is one consideration, there is a specific list of other considerations that the court "shall consider" when setting a bond amount for a domestic violence defendant in Oklahoma.[43] Similar rules apply in Washington and Idaho.

Some of the mandatory considerations on the list in Oklahoma are self-explanatory. These include whether the defendant has a history of domestic violence, a history of other violent acts, and the severity of the alleged violence.

A history of domestic violence includes batterers with a history of charges being dismissed due to lack of cooperation by prior victims. Other items on the list can be more significant than they might appear at first glance. For example, dealing with violating court orders can apply if the defendant was ordered to have no contact with the victim, or past victims, and made contact anyway.

Another example is whether the batterer has exhibited obsessive or controlling behaviors toward the alleged victim. This act is consistent with typical batterer behavior and relates to the power and control dynamics of abusive relationships. That such evidence "shall be" considered by the court when setting bond is very important when cases like Tommy Castro come along.

In Washington, the list of considerations includes whether the accused will seek to intimidate witnesses or otherwise unlawfully interfere with the administration of justice.[44] In Idaho, the list of considerations includes ten (10) factors which include the defendant's character and reputation, the nature of the current charge, and aggravating circumstances that may bear on the likelihood of conviction or possible penalty, and any facts indicating the possibility of violations of the law if the defendant is released without restrictions.[45]

A second helpful statute deals with the Forfeiture by Wrongdoing doctrine. Oklahoma, Washington, and Idaho's codified Forfeiture by Wrongdoing in their evidence codes has a hearsay exception.[46] For a domestic violence prosecutor that is helpful because relying on a binding statute is preferable than relying on persuasive, but not binding, case law.

Forfeiture by Wrongdoing is the doctrine that allows a prosecutor to admit statements from a witness, including a victim, if that witness is unavailable due to wrongful acts or acquiescence of the defendant that caused that person to be unavailable. The idea behind the doctrine is that a defendant should not be able to benefit from such wrongful conduct by objecting to that witness' statements being admitted. Forfeiture by Wrongdoing is hard to prove and is rarely used but is potent when the opportunity presents itself. I would encourage newer domestic violence prosecutors to examine their state's evidence code to see if their state also has a codified Forfeiture by Wrongdoing statute.

A third helpful statute pertains to domestic violence expert witnesses. These experts explain and educate the jury about typical domestic violence victim behavior and reasons why victims are often uncooperative. One potential obstacle a prosecutor may face in a case where a domestic violence expert would be helpful is a *Daubert* challenge.[47] A *Daubert* challenge is an action by the defense, which may be brought either before or during trial, to exclude expert testimony that is not reliable or sufficiently scientific or accepted within its own field.

Daubert is the federal standard for admissibility of expert testimony but was adopted by Oklahoma in 1995.[48] If the defense raises a *Daubert* challenge, then that prosecutor must show that expert testimony regarding victim behavior meets the *Daubert* standard. In Oklahoma, however, the legislature has extinguished that obstacle in domestic violence cases by codifying that testimony by an expert witness about victim behavior in a domestic abuse case *shall* be admissible.[49]

Neither Washington nor Idaho has a similar statute. The courts in each of those states, however, have issued rulings supporting admission of domestic violence expert testimony to explain counterintuitive victim behavior in domestic violence cases.[50]

Another helpful and important statute that newer prosecutors may not be aware of deals with probation violations. Explaining this statute requires a bit of context. One form of probation in Oklahoma is called a suspended sentence. This is where a defendant was convicted and sentenced to some term of incarceration, but the execution of the sentence was suspended in whole or in part by the court, whereby that defendant is released into the community subject to certain court imposed rules and conditions.[51] In the event the defendant violates the rules and conditions of their suspended sentence, the state can file a petition setting forth the grounds for revocation (also called a motion to revoke) of that defendant's suspended sentence and seek to have that defendant incarcerated.[52]

Once such a petition is filed, the defendant has a right to a hearing where competent evidence justifying the revocation must be presented.[53]

An important aspect of revocations is that they are held to different standards than new criminal charges in two key areas.

The first is that, under Oklahoma law, the evidence code does not apply to revocation hearings.[54] This allows the State to introduce some types of evidence that would not be admissible in a criminal trial.

The second is that, under Oklahoma law, the burden of proof for probation revocation is "preponderance of the evidence," which is a much lower burden of proof than the "beyond a reasonable doubt" standard that applies in a criminal trial.[55] Like Oklahoma, the rules of evidence do not apply to proceedings revoking probation in Idaho.[56]

One such case that I prosecuted involved a defendant named Kenute McAnuff, Jr. During my time as a domestic violence prosecutor in Oklahoma, Kenute McAnuff, Jr. may have been the most dangerous batterer I prosecuted. I prosecuted him twice.

The first time I prosecuted him began in December of 2012.[57] He was charged with Domestic Assault and Battery Resulting in Great Bodily Harm. The assault took place in the parking lot in front of a local business. Although the victim received serious injuries, she was spared additional potential injuries because employees of the business came to her aid, chased him away, called 911, and escorted her into the business to wait for EMS and the police to arrive. Before the employees chased him away, McAnuff struck the victim hard enough to fracture bones in her face. At the time, she was pregnant with his child.[58]

There are several facts that make my first case against him particularly memorable. One of them was that, after the employees chased him away, he ran to another local business and tried to hide in the crawl space underneath the floor, where he was subsequently cornered by the police. The responding officers, whose body cameras were on, called to him that if he did not come out, they were going to send the police K-9 unit in to get him. He came out. The other fact was that he was a Jamaican National. At his attorney's request, I had to report his arrest and criminal charges to the Jamaican Consulate pursuant to Article 36 subsection (b) of the 1963 Vienna Convention on Consular Relations.

The State's case against Kenute McAnuff, Jr. was strong, thanks in large part to the assistance and cooperation of the people who went to the victim's aid. In October of 2013 we reached a plea agreement. He entered a plea of no contest and was sentenced to ten years in prison with all but 180 days suspended. He was also given credit for time already served in the Pontotoc County Jail. Since he had already been in jail for more than 180 days, he was released to begin the suspended portion of his sentence on the day he entered his plea. The terms and conditions of his suspended sentence included that he was to have no contact with the victim unless otherwise ordered by the court and that he had to complete the domestic violence batterer's treatment program.

One of the reasons, and perhaps the primary reason, I agreed to that sentence was because I expected him to get deported because of his felony conviction. At the time he entered his plea, he insisted that he would return to Jamaica voluntarily to avoid deportation. I was not persuaded by that, but I did believe that he would be deported regardless. I provided all the pertinent documents about his charges and conviction to the appropriate federal agency within days of his plea and sentencing. For reasons that completely escape me, he was never deported, and continued to live in the area until he reoffended. That did not take long.

I charged Kenute McAnuff, Jr., with Domestic Assault and Battery Second and Subsequent in February of 2014.[59] I also filed a Motion to Revoke his suspended sentence. He had found a new girlfriend and had started abusing her. The abuse was discovered and reported by the victim's parents after they noticed bruising and injuries. Since he was not caught or arrested within 72 hours of the initial report to the Pontotoc County Sheriff's Office, a warrant was issued for his arrest, with a bond set at $100,000.

While meeting with the victim after the case was filed, I learned that the abuse had been ongoing. It appeared that he had learned from his previous case where he was caught because he abused that victim in a public setting. The new victim explained to me how he would force her to take excessive doses of her sleep aids after incidents of physical abuse to keep her out of public view until the bruises healed. That was when it became clear to me just how dangerous he was. After that conversation, there was no doubt in my mind

45

that Kenute McAnuff, Jr. would likely kill his next victim to hide his abuse.

In early March of 2014, he was located and arrested on the outstanding warrant. When he made his initial appearance before the Pontotoc County Special Judge, I announced that the State would not waive the 20-day time requirement on the Motion to Revoke.[60] He entered a plea of no contest to the new charge and the Motion to Revoke nineteen days later, one day shy of the deadline. His suspended sentence was revoked in full. He was also sentenced to the maximum of four years in prison for the new charge, with both sentences running concurrently. From the date of the actual assault to the date he was sentenced was a span of just 38 days. There was no preliminary hearing. There was no trial. There really were no plea negotiations either. He proved himself to be a vicious and dangerous individual, so I put him in prison as fast as the law would allow.

Criminal Defense 101

A few years before I started writing this book, I had a conversation about domestic violence cases with one of the better criminal defense attorneys practicing in Pontotoc County. During that conversation, he said something to me that really stuck with me. He told me that claiming self-defense in domestic violence cases was "criminal defense 101." That comment stuck with me because it put me on notice that if I wanted to truly succeed as a domestic violence prosecutor, I needed to learn how to defeat those claims.

This section will give some background about how self-defense works in a criminal case. In Oklahoma, the lawful use of force or violence upon another, including the use of force or violence for self-defense, was codified in 1998.[61] That statute legalizes the use of non-deadly force upon another to prevent certain offenses against a person or their property provided that the use of force is "not more than sufficient to prevent such offense." The process for raising self-defense and the burden of proof for self-defense, however, are based on case law. To raise self-defense at trial, the defendant must come forward with sufficient evidence to raise it as an issue.[62] Once the issue is raised, the State bears the burden to prove beyond a reasonable doubt that the defendant was NOT acting in self-defense.[63] Whether sufficient evidence is presented to raise self-defense is a question of law for the trial judge.[64] Also, self-defense is not available to a person who is the aggressor or who enters into mutual combat.[65] While they are not identical in all respects, the defenses of self-defense work similarly in Washington and Idaho.

For a domestic violence prosecutor trying a case with an uncooperative victim, this can be a very difficult burden to overcome. In domestic violence cases where a defendant claims self-defense, an uncooperative victim is likely to testify that she was the aggressor in support of the defendant's claim. Such testimony from the victim will satisfy the defense's burden to raise the defense without the defendant or any defense witnesses testifying. That is a tough situation for a prosecutor to be in. In such cases, though, all is not lost. There are two ways to overcome a self-defense claim with an uncooperative victim. First, if the State's case contains sufficient evidence to corroborate the victim's original claim of abuse, then there should be proof beyond a reasonable doubt that the defendant was NOT acting in self-defense.

The next three chapters contain in-depth discussion regarding how to build a strong enough case to overcome that burden. Second, if the State can prove that the defendant used more force or violence than was necessary or reasonable to prevent the offense, then the self-defense claim should fail.

Successfully overcoming a self-defense claim in a domestic violence trial with an uncooperative victim is an example of how a strong understanding of the applicable law can positively affect the outcome of a case. Conversely, if a prosecutor goes to trial in such a case without a strong understanding of how self-defense works, then that prosecutor's chances for a conviction are low. I had the opportunity to sit in the gallery and observe such a trial.[66] The trial I observed did not take place in Oklahoma, Washington, or Idaho, but the self-defense laws in the state where it took place were similar.

Here are the facts of the case for the trial I watched. The victim was a woman, and the defendant was a man. They were in an intimate partner relationship and lived together. Several minor children lived in the home as well. The oldest, the victim's daughter, was a teenager. The other children were much younger.

On the evening of the incident, the defendant was lying on the couch. For reasons that were never brought out at trial, one of the smaller children poured some water on the defendant. The defendant got up and was angry. An argument ensued in the living room. The defendant left the living room and went into a bathroom, shoving the victim onto the couch on his way out. The victim followed the defendant into the bathroom to continue the argument. The teenage daughter took the smaller children into a bedroom and closed the door.

In the bathroom, the defendant was trying to use the faucet. The victim kept turning it off each time the defendant turned it on. The victim was also using her hip to push the defendant sideways. This action was described during testimony as "hip-checking." The victim also threw the defendant's phone out of the bathroom.

The defendant reacted to the victim's provocations by restraining her forcibly against one of the walls in the bathroom. This caused a scratch on the victim below her chin and near her collar bone area. A photograph of the scratch was admitted as evidence.

From there, the defendant grabbed ahold of the victim in a manner described during testimony as a "bear hug" and threw her to the ground with him landing on top of her. This act caused a tear in the victim's shirt. The tear started at the collar and ran down vertically about four or five inches. A photograph of the torn shirt was also admitted as evidence.

Through testimony, it was established that the victim's knee was injured when she was taken to the ground. The injury was serious enough that the victim had trouble walking or putting normal pressure on that knee for the remainder of that day and was still feeling pain the following day. The defendant held the victim on the floor until the daughter arrived.

The daughter testified that she heard a "loud crash," which caused her to leave the bedroom where she had taken the smaller children. She went to the garage, obtained a golf club, and went to the bathroom where she saw the defendant on top of the victim. At some point after hearing the loud crash and before arriving at the bathroom, the daughter also called 911. She had a phone in one hand and the golf club in the other when she arrived at the bathroom door.

On the day of trial, the defendant was facing two counts of domestic abuse. The first count was for restraining the victim against the wall. The second count was for the "bear hug" and throwing the victim to the floor. The victim was uncooperative. She recanted some of what she told the police and did quite a bit of minimizing. Her testimony provided a sufficient basis for the defendant to raise self-defense. During closing arguments, the defense argued self-defense. That was the point where things went south for the prosecutor.

After the defense concluded their argument that the defendant acted in self-defense, it was time for the prosecutor to respond and argue why the defendant was not acting in self-defense. The prosecutor was unprepared to make that argument. It was clear to me that the prosecutor was not well-versed in how self-defense works. At one point, the prosecutor tried to argue to the judge that the defense had given no prior notice that they would raise self-defense. As the judge correctly informed the prosecutor, the defense has no obligation to give any advanced notice that they plan to raise self-defense during the trial, and it is the prosecutor's responsibility to anticipate a self-defense claim. The prosecutor was clearly not aware of that. That is likely why the prosecutor was unprepared to respond and argue against the self-defense claim.

Another problem for the prosecutor was that, due to the victim's aggressive behavior in the bathroom, the defendant did have a right to act in self-defense to a limited degree. There was no means for the prosecutor to prove beyond a reasonable doubt that the defendant was not acting in self-defense. The only viable option for the prosecutor was to argue that the defendant used more force or violence than was necessary to prevent the offense. The prosecutor never made any such argument, however. Based on that, it appeared to me that the prosecutor was also unaware of the limits the law places on use of force in self-defense. The defendant was acquitted on both counts.

In my opinion, and based on my experience, here is what the prosecutor should have done. First, the case should have been charged as one count of domestic abuse instead of two counts. This goes back to case evaluation that I talked about in Chapter One. By trying to split a single altercation into two distinct assaults, the case was overcharged. Second, the facts pertaining to the first count should have been used to satisfy the self-defense claim that was certain to be raised. Third, the facts pertaining to the second count should have been presented as exceeding the limits placed on self-defense.

The argument I would have made is that the defendant was within his legal right to restrain the victim against the wall, but nothing more. At that point, the defendant was out of danger, the victim was restrained, the victim had no further access to the defendant's phone, and there was a clear path for the defendant to exit the bathroom safely. I would have further argued that grabbing the victim in a "bear hug," throwing her to the floor, tearing her shirt, injuring her knee, and keeping her there until the daughter showed up with a phone in one hand and a golf club in the other was far more than necessary or reasonable to prevent any offense committed by the victim. I also would have emphasized that the daughter felt the need to go to the garage and get a golf club.

The prosecutor was clearly new and did not appear to have a great deal of trial experience. There is nothing wrong with that. I was a new prosecutor at one time as well. When the defense argued self-defense in their closing, the prosecutor was blind-sided. It reminded me of the case from Chapter One where the defense attorney had a stack of police reports sitting in front of him. I was blind-sided in that case. Any new domestic violence prosecutor is going to learn a few lessons the hard way and take some lumps along the way. Thus, it is not my intent to be critical of the prosecutor, but rather to illustrate the importance of knowing how self-defense works. I cannot say with any certainty what would have happened if the prosecutor had presented the case in the manner I would have. Perhaps I would have been successful and perhaps not. I can say with certainty, however, that my chances of success would have been much higher because I would have had the law on my side.

Domestic violence victims are not always uncooperative. In my experience, a domestic violence case with a cooperative victim is less likely to go to trial. When they do though, a claim of self-defense can still be a powerful tool for the defense, and so the attorney will likely give it a shot. If the victim is cooperating with the prosecution though, the defense will need to find a different source for the requisite evidence to raise self-defense. A prosecutor in this situation may find that the law is on his side.

In my experience, most domestic abuse cases involve assaults that take place in a private setting. That is not always the case. I have prosecuted numerous cases where there were other witnesses. If the defendant has a third-party witness testify that he was acting in self-defense, then the prosecutor will have to either prove there was no self-defense or prove there was excessive force. The question now is, when there are no third-party witnesses who can help the defendant raise self-defense, what other sources can the defense tap into for the requisite evidence to raise self-defense?

One approach I have dealt with in this situation is the attempted use of character witnesses to raise self-defense. That approach entails the defendant trying to line up some of his friends and family to testify about the victim's propensity for violence during the relationship. It amounts to trying to put the victim on trial. These witnesses will testify about how they know the defendant and have witnessed situations where the defendant and the victim had arguments or physical altercations and, naturally, will testify that it was always the victim who behaved violently or caused the problems. Typically, these witnesses will also try to include claims that the victim is an addict or abuses pills or alcohol or something along those lines. The reason that the prosecutor may have the law on their side in this situation is because some of that character evidence should be inadmissible.[67]

Some additional background information about the admissibility of character evidence is necessary at this point. Evidence of a pertinent trait of character of the victim of a crime offered by the accused is admissible.[68] It is very important that this type of evidence is limited to a "pertinent" trait of character. Also, Evidence of other crimes, wrongs, or acts is not admissible to prove the character of a person to show action in conformity therewith.[69] This rule is typically applied to prevent a prosecutor from arguing that a defendant must be guilty of the charged crime because of past crimes. The rule is not limited to defendants, however. It applies to any person whose character may be an issue, including the victim.

During a domestic violence trial where the defense seeks to assert self-defense, the "trait of character" they will often introduce is the victim's propensity for violent behavior. There is a way to block this strategy. First, this propensity does not become "pertinent" until and unless self-defense is raised.

Second, testimony about the victim's past violent acts cannot be used to prove that the victim behaved violently toward the defendant until and unless self-defense is raised. Only then can the defense character witnesses testify about the victim's propensity for violence. Additionally, in most states, including Washington and Idaho, specific instances of the victim's violent conduct are not admissible even if self-defense is raised since it is not an essential element of a defense.[70]

Once it is established that these defense character witnesses cannot testify regarding the victim's propensity for violence or prior violent acts, the defense is in a tight spot. Under these circumstances, the only remaining source for evidence to raise self-defense is the defendant himself. Any time he can be boxed in so that his self-defense claim requires that he testify and be subject to cross-examination, it may be enough for the defendant to rethink his decision to go to trial at all. Any time a prosecutor can compel a defendant to waive his right to a trial and take a deal by winning on a question of law; clearly that prosecutor has the law on their side.

I'm Sensing a Pattern

The domestic violence statutes in Oklahoma, Washington, and Idaho are not perfect. I'm sure that is true in every other state as well. Perhaps there is a statute that is too narrow. Perhaps there is one that is too broad or vague. Perhaps there is no statute pertaining to a situation that needs one.

When any of these situations arise, it is hard to have the law on your side, but it does not have to be a permanent obstacle. The solution, potentially, can be for the hindered prosecutor to work with their statewide prosecuting agency to submit proposed legislation.[71] If the proposed legislation is drafted properly and is submitted with a sound explanation for why it is necessary, then there is a chance that it will pass. Obviously not every legislative proposal passes, or even makes it to the legislature, but it happens enough that an individual prosecutor should at least consider giving it a try when the need arises.

I ran into one such situation regarding a statute that was too narrow. Oklahoma had a statute titled Domestic Abuse with Prior Pattern of Physical Abuse, which is a felony.[72] The version of that statute that was in effect when I started out defined a prior pattern of physical abuse as "three or more separate incidences, occurring on different days, where all incidences occurred within the previous six-month period, and each incident relates to an act constituting assault and battery or domestic abuse committed by the defendant... where proof is established by the sworn testimony of a third party who was a witness to the alleged physical abuse or by other admissible direct evidence that is independent of the testimony of the victim."[73] The purpose of the statute was to create a means whereby a batterer that had not previously been convicted of domestic abuse could be treated as a repeat offender when it was warranted by the evidence to do so. The basis for such a statute is sound because domestic abuse often goes unreported.

For the majority of my first three years working in Oklahoma, I was aware of the statute. When I was presented with new domestic violence cases that included evidence of prior abuse I would look to see if the prior abuse fit the requirements of a prior pattern of physical abuse. I never really came close. Each time I thought I might have a case where there was a sufficient prior pattern it would turn out that I either lacked the requisite number of separate incidences, that the prior incidences were outside of the requisite six-month timeframe, or both.

While the statute's purpose was sound, its language was just too narrow. Instead of giving up on ever using the statute I decided to try and change it. I received the email from the District Attorney's Council in 2013 requesting that any proposed legislative changes be submitted for review. That August, I drafted my proposal to amend the statute and broaden the definition of a prior pattern. My proposal called for a prior pattern to be defined as "three or more separate incidences, including the present offense, occurring on different days, where all incidences occurred within the previous twelve-month period, and each incident relates to an act constituting assault and battery or domestic abuse committed by the defendant." My proposal increased the requisite time frame to twelve months and reduced the requisite number of incidents from four to three.

After my proposed changes were submitted and reviewed by the District Attorney's Council, they were approved to be included in the legislative package that was submitted to the legislature. The legislature passed the proposed change. Effective November 1, 2014, my proposed changes went into effect as law.[74] In the grand scheme of things, the successful codification of my proposed legislative change is not that big of a deal. While it may not have been anything earth shattering, I am still proud of it because it worked. I was able to prosecute someone for violating a law that I wrote, and that was cool.[75] I encourage any domestic violence prosecutor to try to change any statute that is problematic, because you are likely to have that law on your side if you are the one who wrote it.

Hitting Back

CHAPTER THREE

Have the Facts on Your Side

Domestic violence victims are often uncooperative with law enforcement and the prosecution. This creates several problems for the people working to hold batterers accountable.

The first problem is that it can make evidence collection more difficult. I address this aspect of uncooperative victims in chapter five.

The second problem is that uncooperative victims make it more difficult to succeed in the courtroom. This difficulty manifests itself in one of two ways. The first manifestation is a victim who is giving testimony favorable to the defense. This could entail a different version of events than what she originally reported, or a recantation of her original claims. The second manifestation is a victim who is absent from court entirely. This chapter discusses several approaches that a prosecutor can use to overcome these problems in the courtroom, and that the prosecutor's chances for success are much greater if they have the facts on their side.

Technology is Your Friend

There is no doubt that modern technology gives a domestic violence prosecutor a greater chance to overcome an uncooperative or absent victim in the courtroom. The use of technology matters even more considering the landmark Supreme Court decision in *Crawford v. Washington* and its progeny, which made victimless prosecution much more difficult for prosecutors.[76] The effective use of available technology can assist a prosecutor by making it more difficult for a victim to recant, making it difficult for an uncooperative victim to reconcile her pro-defense testimony with the evidence, and in the event of an absent victim, by allowing the prosecutor to essentially bring the victim into the courtroom to testify even though the victim is not physically present. The various forms of helpful technology include recorded 911 phone calls, recorded jail phone calls, and body camera video recordings.

911 recordings often contain useful evidence, including both circumstantial and direct. Useful circumstantial evidence can include the fact that either the victim or a third party saw a need to place an emergency call in the first place. People do not typically call 911 without a good reason, and so the call's very existence may support the prosecutor's case. Additional circumstantial evidence that a 911 call may include is the caller's tone and emotional state and any sounds emanating from the background.

When the victim is the caller and is obviously crying, having difficulty speaking clearly, and is distressed, that is all circumstantial evidence that can potentially help the prosecutor, especially if the victim's testimony includes efforts to minimize. The same is true if a third-party caller sounds frantic or distressed. Also, a 911 call may contain shouts or other distinct sounds of a struggle or altercation going on while the caller is talking to the dispatcher. In a case where the contents of a 911 call are consistent with a serious or physical incident it can be hard for a minimizing or recanting victim to reconcile their testimony with the recording.

The contents of a 911 call typically contain useful direct evidence as well. The direct evidence includes the caller's description of the incident. A recorded statement where the caller, whether it is the victim or a third-party, describes the assault is obviously significant. Additionally, specific details from a 911 call can sometimes be corroborated and connected to evidence found at the scene by law enforcement. For example, if a victim makes a 911 call and describes how she locked herself into the bathroom and the batterer forced entry then evidence of forced entry through the bathroom door becomes much more potent.

If the victim in such a case were to testify that the incident did not happen or was merely a verbal argument, then that victim would have a difficult time reconciling her testimony with the 911 call and the signs of forced entry on the bathroom door. Sometimes, the 911 recording may include spontaneous and incriminating background statements made by the defendant. Such statements are also significant.

Regardless of how helpful a 911 recording might be, the prosecutor still must first admit the recording as evidence. A 911 recording can be subject to challenge on several grounds. One challenge I have run into is that the recording is cumulative. This challenge is more likely to arise in cases where the victim made the call and is cooperative or a third-party caller made the call and is present in court to testify. In either situation, I typically did not bother trying to admit the recording unless there was helpful background evidence.

When the recording contains evidence, such as sounds of a physical altercation or incriminating statements by the defendant, it should be easy for the prosecutor to overcome any cumulative objections since that evidence is distinguishable from the caller's statements to the dispatcher.

Additionally, if the victim was the caller and is testifying as an uncooperative witness, then her testimony will likely conflict with the contents of the recording. That should also make it easy for the prosecutor to overcome a cumulative objection. If the victim made the call and is testifying, but is trying to minimize, the cumulative objection can be a problem because the victim's testimony might not diverge from her statements in the recording. When this happens, it is important to remember that the rule against cumulative evidence applies to cumulative evidence that is "needless."[77] If the prosecutor can articulate a reasonable need to admit the recording, then that should defeat the objection.

In a situation with a minimizing victim, that need might be to present her emotional state or apparent distress in the recording as a contrast to her testimony. One piece of advice I want to emphasize for any prosecutors or law enforcement investigators reading this is that it is a good idea to pay close attention to anything going on in the background of a 911 recording.

Another basis for challenging a 911 recording is that it is inadmissible hearsay. This challenge is likely to arise if the caller is not present in court to testify or if the recording contains audible third-party comments in the background that are significant. Any 911 call obviously contains out of court statements. If a prosecutor wants to admit the recording in court, then the contents are likely being offered, in whole or in part, to prove the truth of the matter asserted; therefore, it is likely that the contents of the recording fall within the hearsay definition.[78] To admit the recording there must be an applicable hearsay exception or exclusion. Potential hearsay exceptions that may work include the "present sense impression" exception, the "excited utterance" exception, and the "state of mind" exception[79]. One problem with using any of those three exceptions is that none of them apply to the entire recording. Instead, each individual statement within the recording, including any background statements, is subject to its own challenge and analysis. Thus, if a 911 recording has multiple statements from multiple people, there is a potential quagmire of objections and arguments where each individual statement from each person is subject to its own analysis. The result can be a situation where some statements are ruled admissible while other statements are not.

In Oklahoma, that is not my preferred approach. Instead, I rely on the "business record" exception and the "public record" exception to the hearsay rule.[80] In my opinion, either of those exceptions can apply to a 911 recording based on how they are worded in Oklahoma. When I was faced with a hearsay objection to a 911 recording, I typically cited both exceptions in my response. After I asked the necessary foundational questions, I was always successful. The reason I preferred this approach is that the business record and public record exceptions apply to the entire recording instead of individual statements. As a result, I avoided any potential quagmires. Neither Washington nor Idaho allowed 911 recordings into evidence as business records or public records. All 911 calls I tried to admit in Washington or Idaho were analyzed statement by statement.

Once the hearsay challenge is overcome, there may be one more hurdle to clear. The 911 recording may be challenged on grounds of confrontation. Obviously, this is not a hurdle if the caller is available to testify; however, in a domestic violence case with an absent victim, where the victim was the caller, a confrontation objection is likely. In the wake of the *Crawford* decision and its progeny, whether the Confrontation Clause applies to a 911 recording depends on whether the contents are testimonial. The *Crawford* decision established that prior testimonial statements of witnesses could not be admitted without cross examination. *Crawford* also established that testimonial statements include "statements made under circumstances which would lead an objective witness to reasonably believe that such statement would be available for use at a later trial."[81] Subsequently, the Supreme Court addressed how its *Crawford* decision should be applied to a 911 recording. In the case of *Davis v. Washington,* the Supreme Court held that the primary purpose for the 911 call at issue in that case was to deal with an "ongoing emergency," and therefore the statements were not testimonial.[82]

Clearing the confrontation hurdle may not be as simple as citing the *Davis* case, however. In 2009, for example, the Oklahoma Court of Criminal Appeals held that a 911 recording contained testimonial statements and was improperly admitted by the trial court in violation of the Confrontation Clause.[83] In *Hunt*, the Court noted in footnote number four that the facts were distinguishable from the facts in the *Davis* case. Case law can vary from state to state, so other states may have a different precedent than Oklahoma. Regardless, the *Hunt* decision should still put a domestic violence prosecutor on notice that admitting a 911 call made by an absent victim will likely require showing how the facts of their case are similar to *Davis*.

One final aspect of 911 calls, or any form of emergency call, that a domestic violence prosecutor should be mindful of is that batterers tend to prevent them or attempt to prevent them. Oklahoma has a statute that criminalizes disrupting or interfering with an emergency call.[84] Most other states likely have a similar statute on their books.

In cases where the batterer disrupted, prevented, or attempted to disrupt or prevent the victim from making an emergency call, that act can strengthen the prosecution's case in several ways. First, it can lead to additional charges or counts if it is a standalone crime. Second, disrupting an emergency call is evidence that the batterer knows he did something wrong.

Disrupted emergency calls are particularly probative when the disruption is caught on the recording. I have prosecuted many cases where the caller told the dispatcher that the batterer was trying to take the phone or prevent the phone call in some way. I have also prosecuted many cases where an emergency call was disrupted, and the recording caught the struggle for the phone before the call ended. In another case, the victim told the police that the batterer took her mobile phone and threw it off the landing outside their second story apartment. The police found her phone on the ground some ninety feet away. Circumstances like these can be very difficult for a batterer to explain while maintaining innocence.

Just a Phone Call Away

In Chapter One, I discussed the significance of recorded inmate jail calls. Like 911 calls, recorded jail calls often contain both direct and circumstantial evidence. One aspect of that distinguishes them from 911 recordings or body camera videos is that they are not available as consistently. There are several reasons for that. First, there are many domestic violence cases, particularly misdemeanors, where the batterer does not spend any significant time (or any time) in jail. Second, some batterers are smart enough to stay off the phones while they are in jail. In cases where the batterer was in jail for at least a full day or more, however, there is a good chance that phone calls were made.

Considering that inmate jail calls are recorded, it is a fair question to ask why it is so common for batterers to get on the phone and make self-incriminating statements. The main reason is they often have no choice. In abusive relationships, the batterer is typically the dominant party and is the architect of the power, control, isolation, and dependency dynamics in the relationship.

When the batterer finds himself stuck in jail, the dynamics become reversed. While incarcerated, the batterer is somewhat isolated and becomes dependent on the victim. The victim becomes the dominant party, and the batterer needs her help to get out of jail.

The only way the batterer can try to convince his victim to help him is to pick up the phone and call her. Also, how else is an uncooperative victim going to try to help the batterer get out of jail besides asking for the charges to be dropped or refusing to testify?

These conversations typically take place within a day or two of the arrest. It is difficult for that conversation to happen without some helpful statements being made. In my experience where the victim asked to have the charges dropped or submitted a yellow pad letter, the likelihood of a useful jail call between the batterer and the victim was very high.

As noted in Chapter One, a useful recording is one that contains statements usable in court. Comments batterers tend to make on recorded jail calls can be roughly divided into two categories.

The first consists of incriminating statements. These are recordings that can be used to help prove that the defendant is guilty. Incriminating statements can be either circumstantial or direct evidence of guilt. Statements that are circumstantial evidence include things like the batterer apologizing for what happened, promising to get help, saying it will not happen again, and so forth.

Direct evidence includes explicit admissions of guilt, or discussion of the facts of the case wherein specific details are corroborated. For example, even if the batterer does not admit to the assault, he may admit that he did take the victim's phone and break it or that he did kick the door open.

In a case where a victim is trying to recant or minimize, and parts of the original version can be corroborated, it becomes harder for the victim to offer a new version that is consistent with the evidence. Also, if the batterer is claiming he did not commit the assault, what is he apologizing for and what does he need help with?

Useful statements do not always come from the batterer. Sometimes the victim makes useful comments. The victim may discuss the nature and severity of her injuries, her physical condition in the aftermath of the assault, or confront the batterer about the incident. If a recorded jail call includes the victim talking about missing work due to her injuries, describing how long it is taking for her injuries to heal, or how she was injured, then that can be helpful. Also, the victim asking her batterer "Why did you do this to me?" or something to that effect, can be helpful.

Questions of that nature place responsibility on the batterer, and such questions often elicit helpful responses. If a victim becomes uncooperative, recants, or minimizes, it can be hard for her to reconcile that with what she said on the phone with her batterer.

The second category of useful statements consists of those where the defendant tries to influence the victim with regards to cooperating or testifying. It is important to note that the two categories are not mutually exclusive. Certain statements can fit into both categories, and a single phone call might include separate statements that fit into each category.

Statements that fit into this category include explicit requests or demands that the victim try to get the charges dropped, explicit requests or demands that the victim avoid talking to the District Attorney's Office or law enforcement, and explicit requests or demands that the victim avoid appearing in court. Statements fitting this category are often not explicit.

Examples of implicit statements include the batterer emphasizing that he might have to stay in jail or go to prison if the charges are not dropped, emphasizing that he will lose his job if he stays in jail or goes to prison, and efforts by the batterer to make the victim feel guilty or responsible for him being in jail. Sometimes these statements will be in the form of questions. I have heard many batterers ask their victim "Why did you call the police on me?"; "Why did you do this to me?"; "Do you want me to go to jail?"; or "Do you want me to lose my job?" Questions like those are meant to persuade the victim to be uncooperative, and they are often very effective.

Statements in the second category can strengthen the prosecutor's case in other ways, including becoming the basis for new charges. Witness tampering is a crime, and the acts constituting witness tampering can be broad. The statute for witness tampering in Oklahoma, for example, is very broad. It applies to "[e]very person who willfully prevents or attempts to prevent any person from giving testimony or producing any record, document or other object, who has been duly summoned or subpoenaed....or who is a witness to any reported crime, or *threatens or procures physical or mental harm through force or fear with the intent to prevent any witness from appearing in court to give his or her testimony* or produce any record, document or other object, *or to alter his or her testimony*" (emphasis added).[85]

As I mentioned in Chapter One, it is rare for a batterer to explicitly threaten additional physical harm in jail call recordings. Thus, with regards to domestic violence, the references to "mental harm" and "through force or fear" are significant. Under Oklahoma law, and under the law of any state with a similar statute, a batterer does not have to make an explicit threat of harm to be guilty of witness tampering. Threats of mental harm through fear will also work. So, when a batterer is on the jail phone attempting to convince his victim to be uncooperative by emphasizing the hardships she will face if he is convicted, must stay in jail, or is sent to prison, then he is tampering. Also, the statute applies to any instance where a batterer tries to get the victim "to alter his or her testimony." A batterer is also tampering when he is attempting to "coach" his victim to adopt a new version of events.

Another significant aspect of the statute is that it applies with regards to "any person" who "is a witness to any reported crime." This language allows the law to apply to acts committed before any charges or indictments are brought or before anything is filed with the court. When a domestic assault talks place, the victim is a witness to it. The moment the assault is reported to law enforcement then the victim becomes a "witness to any reported crime." If that language was absent, then the batterer would have free reign to tamper with his victim up until such time that court documents were filed listing the victim as a State's witness or until she was "duly summoned or subpoenaed." In some cases, that time gap can be days or even weeks. Since the statute contains that broad language, it will apply to any statements in any jail call placed after the assault itself took place.

Helpful jail calls are not always between the batterer and his victim. Sometimes a batterer will call a third party, such as a friend or relative. I have prosecuted cases where the batterer called his parents, for example. In my experience, jail calls to third parties are less likely to include statements that fit into the first category and are more likely to include statements that fit into the second category. I have listened to many recorded jail calls where a batterer and a third party discussed keeping the victim from appearing in court. I would encourage any prosecutor or investigator to pay as much attention to jail phone calls made to third parties as they do to ones made to the victim.

Jail call recordings can also be helpful for cross examination of defense witnesses. In Chapter Two, I discussed one approach to dealing with defense character witnesses. That included preventing batterers from using character witnesses to raise self-defense.

In a domestic violence case with an uncooperative victim, the batterer likely has no need to rely on character witnesses to raise self-defense. Instead, the batterer can rely on his victim to provide the testimony to raise self-defense. Once self-defense is raised, the door opens for character witnesses to testify because testimony regarding the victim's propensity for violent behavior becomes pertinent. In my experience, such character witnesses are often the batterer's parents or someone who is close to the batterer. This is because a character witness must be familiar with the batterer, his victim, and their relationship before they can offer opinion testimony about her propensity for violence. At that point, it can be helpful if there is a recorded jail call between the batterer and witness. In my experience, a call is more likely to exist if the witness is also one of the batterer's parents. If any calls are found that contain any discussion of the case, or that witness' testimony, then the cross examination of that witness should be interesting.

Another type of case where jail call recordings can be helpful is when the victim is absent. *Hammon v. Indiana*, which was decided by the Supreme Court along with the *Davis* case, made victimless prosecution much more difficult for prosecutors. The *Hammon* case arose from a domestic violence case where the victim was absent. The Court held that the victim's statement to police was inadmissible under the Confrontation Clause because it was testimonial.[86] Statements in a recorded jail call between the batterer and his victim, however, are not testimonial. Like a 911 recording made by the victim, a recorded jail call between the batterer and the victim that contains incriminating statements, can be a way to bring her into the courtroom when she is not physically present.

As noted in Chapter One, jail call recordings can also be helpful in absent victim cases by strengthening a Forfeiture by Wrongdoing action. This action can be supported by statements falling into either of the two categories. Also, jail call recordings between the batterer and a third party about preventing the victim from cooperating or appearing in court can help a forfeiture by wrongdoing action. These recordings can include explicit threats or verbal efforts to keep the victim away from court.

Forfeiture by Wrongdoing actions may also be supported by manipulative statements reflecting the batterer's coercive control. These include expressions of love, regret, a desire to change, or an emphasis on keeping the family together.[87]

Like a 911 recording, a helpful jail call recording must be admitted before it can be used. These can be potent pieces of evidence, and any attempt to admit them as evidence will be met with a challenge.

Jail call recordings may be challenged on several grounds. One basis is on privacy or unlawful surveillance grounds. This defense move can involve a claim that either the batterer had a reasonable expectation of privacy that was violated, or the call was recorded without consent in violation of laws prohibiting certain forms of surveillance.

The success or failure of this challenge depends on whether there was an audible warning to both parties that the call was subject to being recorded or monitored. Typically, a jail phone system will, at the beginning of each call, have an automated warning message audible to both parties giving them notice that the call is subject to being recorded or monitored.[88]

Courts at both the state and federal level have repeatedly held that inmates proceeding with a phone call despite the warning have given implied consent to the call being recorded, do not have a reasonable expectation of privacy, and any right to privacy they may have is outweighed by the institution's interest in security.[89]

Another basis for challenging jail call recordings is for lack of foundation. To admit a piece of evidence, the offering party must lay the proper foundation. That means it must show that the piece of evidence is relevant and authentic before the piece of evidence can be admitted.

With regards to a recorded jail call in a domestic violence case with an uncooperative or absent victim, this can be a problem. Part of laying the proper foundation to admit a recorded jail call involves identifying the voices in the recording. If there is no way to show who is talking, then there is no way to show that the recording is relevant to the case being prosecuted. It is unlikely that the batterer is going to take the stand and identify his own voice. If the victim or third-party recipient is present but uncooperative, they may not give the necessary answers to identify the voices. If the victim or third-party recipient is absent, then the prosecutor cannot even try to ask them. Fortunately, there are other means by which a prosecutor might be able to lay the necessary foundation.

First, the prosecutor can rely on jail records to help lay the proper foundation. When recordings are pulled from the jail phone system, the data typically includes both the recording as well as a record of when each call was made, which specific phone was used, the number dialed, the number of calls made, and which inmate placed each call.

Booking records from the jail should also be available to show when the batterer was booked into and out of the jail. In some cases, it may be possible to obtain surveillance video of the jail phones with date and time stamps that can be matched with the jail phone records. These can help the prosecutor lay the proper foundation in several ways. First, the prosecutor can establish that the call was made while the batterer was incarcerated. Additionally, with the help of either the investigating officer or a third party, the prosecutor can likely show that the call was made to the victim's phone number. This can be shown by having the investigating officer or third party testify that they have used that same number to successfully contact the victim. If neither the investigating officer nor a third-party witness are able to give that testimony, which could happen if the officer called but the victim never answered, then it may be necessary to obtain phone records for the number called which may connect that phone number to the victim.

Also, it is not safe to assume that the phone is in the victim's name. The phone may be in the batterer's name. If the victim is a young woman, lives at home, or is in college, then her phone might be attached to her parents' account. I have prosecuted cases where the victim was uncooperative, but her phone was attached to her parents' account, and her parents were more than happy to provide phone records. If there were numerous calls made from the jail to the victim's number while the batterer was in jail, then a strong argument can be made that the batterer was the caller.

Finally, if there is surveillance footage showing the batterer using the phone while the phone was used to call the victim's number, then that is definitive proof that the batterer's voice is one of the voices in the recording.

As I mentioned, the jail call records typically indicate which inmate placed each call. This is often accomplished by requiring the inmates to enter a personal identification number (PIN) or other identifying access code, which in turn identifies that inmate as the caller. One problem with this is that inmates often share or trade their PIN or access code. I dealt with many instances where a record of all jail calls made to the victim's phone number showed calls made by numerous different inmates.

Typically, in such instances, the batterer's name did not appear anywhere in the record. Fortunately, this is an easy issue to overcome, and can even be helpful. The fact that the batterer always used another inmate's name when calling the victim can be used to show that he was trying to conceal the conversations.

If that same batterer used his own PIN or access code to place calls to other people, then the argument that he was trying to conceal his conversations with the victim is even stronger.

An effective way to overcome this problem is with an "offer of proof" that the caller has the same voice in all the calls.[90] In the absence of a witness who can identify either party in a jail call recording, the prosecutor may be able to provide a list of calls made to the victim's number where the voices were the same. This includes instances where the caller tried to conceal his identity by using other inmates' names.

In response to a foundation challenge, the prosecutor can also use helpful contents of the recording as the foundation for its admissibility. For example, if either the caller or the recipient refers to themselves, or each other, by name then that can be included in the offer of proof.

Other examples include any conversation about the case, such as references to matching court dates or references to specific details that correlate to details of that case. If the batterer was arrested on a weekend and is scheduled to appear before the court on Monday and a recorded jail call to the victim that Sunday includes the caller talking about "seeing the judge tomorrow" then that is helpful. Also, if the caller tells the recipient how much he loves her and how much he wants to be back "home" with her, then that is also helpful. Thus, even without a witness who can identify the parties, the call records and an offer of proof should be more than enough to overcome any foundation challenge.

Jail call recordings can also be challenged on hearsay grounds. Like 911 recordings, the contents of these recordings fall within the hearsay definition.[91] Thus, there must be an applicable hearsay exception or exclusion. Like with 911 recordings, an effective approach would be to cite the "business record" and "public record" exceptions since these apply to the entire recording instead of to specific individual statements within a recording.[92]

The "public record" exception has exceptions of its own. There are certain types of evidence that might fit the definition of a "public record" and still not be admissible. Examples include police reports and certain factual findings.[93] Jail call recordings do not fit any of the exceptions under the "public records" exception because, even though a government agency created the recording, the caller is primarily responsible for creating the content by placing the call in the first place and typically no government agents or officials participated in the call. There is just no way for a jail phone call to constitute a police report or a factual finding of any kind. Provided I laid the proper foundation, I was always successful with this approach in Oklahoma.

If, for any reason, neither the "business record" nor "public record" exceptions succeed in defeating a hearsay challenge, there are other options. In both Washington and Idaho, these other options were necessary.

First, any of the batterer's statements in a recorded jail call are not hearsay since they are his own statements and are being used against him. Such statements are explicitly excluded from the hearsay definition.[94] At the very least, the batterer's side of the recorded conversations should be admissible. That leaves only the statements from the recipient at issue, and each individual statement must qualify for one or more hearsay exceptions to be admissible. For example, if the batterer and victim get into a heated argument, then the "present sense impression" or "excited utterance" exceptions may apply to some of the statements made during the argument.[95] Also, if the call is placed shortly after the assault, then statements made by the victim may still constitute "excited utterances" if the victim is still clearly under the stress of the assault. This can be messy because the result can be a recorded jail call where some of the recipient's statements are admissible while other statements are not.

Additional challenges I have encountered are claims that conversations are privileged between spouses, that the probative value of the recordings are outweighed by the danger of unfair prejudice, and that admission of the recordings violates the batterer's *Miranda* rights.

Oklahoma law, like other state laws and federal laws, recognizes a privilege for spouses that limit when one spouse can repeat private statements made by the other spouse.[96] This has exceptions. A privilege challenge should fail in a case where the batterer and his victim are a married couple because spousal privileges do not typically apply in criminal cases where one spouse is charged with a crime against the other.[97]

The unfair prejudice challenge should also be easy to overcome. It is important to understand the correct standard for this challenge. The standard is often incorrectly stated to be that a piece of evidence is inadmissible if its probative value is outweighed or substantially outweighed by its prejudicial effect. That is incorrect. The correct standard is that evidence is inadmissible if its probative value is substantially outweighed by the danger of unfair prejudice.[98] The key word in the correct standard is "unfair."

All evidence is prejudicial, otherwise it would probably be irrelevant. The issue with this challenge is whether the prejudice is unfair. It is not. There is nothing unfair about using a batterer's own words against him, especially when taken from a recorded call that the batterer chose to make in the first place. Finally, the *Miranda* challenge should be easy to overcome since *Miranda* applies to custodial interrogations, and any jail calls that the batterer chooses to make are in no way interrogations.[99]

I Can See Again

In one case I prosecuted, I was faced with a victim that was both uncooperative and absent.[100] The circumstances of this case illustrate several of the topics I have discussed so far, including yellow pad letters, the evidentiary value of jail call recordings, overcoming challenges to jail call recordings, and an absent victim. The case arose from a domestic assault by a man against his wife. It was a felony because the batterer had an applicable prior domestic violence and other felony convictions and had served time in prison.

Because of his criminal history, his bond was high, and he was unable to bond out of jail. One aspect of this case that sets it apart from other cases with uncooperative victims was that, during the time in which this case was being prosecuted, the victim was battling terminal cancer.

From the outset of the case, the victim was uncooperative. She made multiple visits to my office to meet about why she wanted the charges dropped. On one of her visits, she brought with her a small basket holding an array of prescription pill bottles. She told me that she brought all her medications with her because she was ready to be taken to jail for filing a false police report. She was not taken to jail. On each visit, she also provided me with a yellow pad letter. She wrote some of the letters in our lobby and wrote some of them at home and brought them with her. All the letters

79

were dated.

I received this case well after my return from the Portland conference. Thus, as had become my usual practice when I received a yellow-pad letter, I requested the recordings of any phone calls made from the jail to the victim's phone number. The batterer was arrested on a weekend. He saw the judge on the following Monday. That was when he learned his bond amount.

The phone calls started the next day. To describe them as merely "helpful" would be an understatement. During the conversations, the batterer used a great deal of foul language, called the victim ugly names, and made a lot of other ugly and degrading remarks. He also made numerous admissions of guilt. While the explicit admissions of guilt were the most helpful statements made, a close second were the explicit threats and efforts to prevent the victim from appearing in court or cooperating.

This is where the dates on the yellow-pad letters come in. During several of the phone calls, the batterer instructed the victim on what to write or what to say to the District Attorney's Office. She wrote what he told her to write and then gave me the letters. I read the letters and listened to the phone calls. I was then able to match them up and put them in order based on the dates on the letters and the dates the calls were made. They all fit perfectly. On one of the calls, which was placed the evening prior to the aforementioned visit to my office, he instructed her to bring all her medications with her, so she would be ready to go to jail for making a false police report. That evidence, combined with the explicit threats, gave rise to additional charges of witness tampering.

Due to her deteriorating health, the victim was unable to appear at the preliminary hearing for this case.[101] I had to proceed with an absent victim. In doing so, I relied heavily on the jail call recordings but had to get them admitted first.

The recordings contained the automated warning, so there were no issues of consent or privacy raised; however, they were challenged both on the grounds of hearsay and lack of foundation. I overcame the hearsay issue by relying on the "public record" exception and showing that the recordings did not constitute any sort of police report or factual finding.

To overcome the foundation challenge, I had to prove whose voices were in the recordings. I overcame that with an offer of proof. Fortunately, the recordings contained many statements that helped identify the participants. My offer of proof included that each call was made while the batterer was in jail, that each call was made to a phone number connected to the victim, that each recording contained the same two voices, that the caller and recipient referred to each other by name, that they discussed specific details of the case including the facts of the case, the State's plea offer, and court dates, and that they discussed specific details of their relationship. The recordings were admitted.

That preliminary hearing remains one of the highlights of my time working in Ada. After the court ruled that the recordings would be admitted, I announced that I had no objection to the Court adjourning the hearing and listening to the recordings in chambers before making a decision instead of playing the recordings aloud in open court. Because there were six different jail calls and they contained a lot of profanity and disturbing content, I was not anticipating any objections. The batterer instructed his attorney to object, however, and insisted that I play the recordings in open court. He had that right, and so the court sustained the objection.

I had my equipment with me just in case, so I played the recordings in open court. There were people in the gallery observing the proceedings when I began playing the recordings. Several of those people were so offended by what they heard that they left the courtroom. One of the people who left was a victim in another felony domestic abuse case that was also set for a preliminary hearing that morning. The batterer in that other case was in the gallery waiting for his preliminary hearing. To this day, I would like to know what was going through his head while he listened to those recordings.

When I was about to start playing the fourth call, the batterer instructed his attorney to withdraw their objection because they had heard enough, to which the judge responded that the Court had also heard enough. The case was bound over for trial. Here are some of the exchanges between that batterer and that victim, with only the names removed, that occurred in those phone calls:

Batterer - What's wrong with you, you got a cold?

Victim - No I'm…I'm still healing. At least the swelling in my brain has gone down and I can see again.

B - What are you talking about?

V - You didn't realize you'd been beatin' me almost non-stop for five days.

B - Nah, I hit you three times [name].

V - No [name], you didn't.

B - Yes.

V- You don't even remember backhanding me and knocking my glasses off into the trash. You thought I threw my glasses away.

B - Don't even…we can't even talk about this on the phone [name].

I have listened to many jail call recordings. In my experience, and a little bit to my surprise, it is quite common for a batterer to not only make helpful statements during a jail call, but then later point out that they should not talk about the case on the phone. Here is another exchange between that batterer and victim from a different call:

B - So what all did this lawyer say, man?

[Several seconds of silence]

B - Can you stop and fucking quit playing Nazi long enough to give me that fucking information, stupid, or what?

V - Okay, you're—

[He cuts her off]

B - You're really pissing me off [name] right now. And this is why you get fucking black eyes and fucking knocked in the fucking head[102].

V - Eight years and seventeen years' probation is the best I can get you on the plea bargain.

B - I'm not, I'm not takin' it. I'm not takin' nothin'. You do not never go to court again; do you understand me? Do you understand me? You do not have a meeting....

V - I understand you.

B - You do not have a meeting with the D.A. ever again. You never go to the courthouse. Do you understand me?

V - I understand.

B - All right, and when [name] gets her hands on you don't fuckin', don't run, just take your ass whoopin' for bein' stupid, alright? When my sister [name] gets her hands on you, take your ass whoopin'.

There are a few final points about those calls that I want to make. First, as I discussed in Chapter One, I prefer to discuss a plea offer with the victim before extending the offer. That is what happened in this case. The plea offer she told him about was consistent with what I was going to offer him. It helped me admit the jail calls that the victim accurately relayed my plea offer. The second point is that these exchanges are not typical. This case is an extreme example of how powerful jail call recordings can be as evidence. Most other cases with helpful jail call recordings lack such vulgarity and ugliness. Considering that I had to proceed without the victim, I caught a break by having a batterer go to such lengths to help me out. A few months after the preliminary hearing, the victim lost her battle with cancer and passed away before the case was resolved. The batterer ended up in prison for his crimes. The outcome of the case was due almost entirely to the jail call recordings. In that case, I not only had the facts on my side, but I also had the batterer on my side.

Worth a Thousand Words

Like 911 recordings and recorded jail calls, body camera video recordings typically contain useful evidence. Because they record audio and video, the list of examples is nearly endless.

Video of the scene is often very compelling. Whether there is furniture out of place, fixtures that fell off the wall, broken dishes, broken furniture, or a door that has been forced open, the ability to see it on video is powerful.

Additionally, video of the people at the scene, including the victim, is often very compelling. Emotions tend to be running high, so there is typically a great deal of raw, unscripted emotion. Recordings normally capture what everyone is saying, even people who may not be speaking to the officer or answering the officer's questions. It is common for a body camera video to capture conversations between third parties. This may include the victim talking to someone else, the victim arguing with the batterer, third party witnesses talking to each other, spontaneous statements by third party witnesses, or spontaneous statements by the batterer.

The victim's emotional state and physical appearance, including visible injuries, are also typically caught by the video. Also, in cases where the batterer fled the scene before police arrived, the video puts an extra spotlight on his absence.

Prior to body cameras, all this evidence had to be presented in court through verbal descriptions by police officers or other witnesses along with still photographs or exhibits. Everyone is familiar with the idea that "a picture is worth a thousand words." Well, how many words is a video worth? Even the best trained and most thorough police officer cannot write a police report about an incident that is as complete and as compelling as a video recording of the scene. Even an officer with extensive experience testifying cannot describe a victim's appearance or a victim's demeanor with as much detail as a video showing her at the scene.

The victim's demeanor, emotional state, and appearance at the time the police first arrive is important because, in most cases, the police arrive shortly after the incident. In my experience, most domestic violence cases are reported to law enforcement during or shortly after the assault. In such cases, the first few minutes after officers arrive capture the victim while she is still in fear for her immediate safety and still under the stress of the assault. In some instances, the victim struggles to speak clearly or answer questions due to the extreme stress of the situation. In those situations, her demeanor alone can be powerful evidence. The video shows a great deal of credibility because there has often been no opportunity for her to think rationally about the situation, fabricate any details, or anything of that nature.

Instead, the contents of the video are raw, unscripted, and the intense emotion on display is genuine. In a case where a victim is later uncooperative, it can be difficult for her to recant or offer a different version of events and reconcile that with the video. Prior to body camera videos, proving a victim's original claim after she either recanted, provided a new version of events, or tried to minimize required relying on still photos, law enforcement testimony, third-party witness testimony, and any statement that the victim wrote out after the fact. None of those are as powerful as a good body camera video.

The county seat of Pontotoc County is the City of Ada. If you happen to be a John Grisham fan, you may have heard of a non-fiction book he wrote about a man who was wrongly convicted of murder in Ada.

In 2010, the Ada Police Department initiated a pilot program for officer-worn body cameras. A small number of officers were issued body cameras to wear while on duty. Shortly thereafter I received the first domestic violence case that included a body camera video. The video contained an uninterrupted audio and visual recording from the time the officer arrived through the officer's departure. My immediate reaction while I watched the video was that, when it comes to prosecuting domestic violence, it was a "game changer." I still feel that way. Instead of being limited to reading written witness statements, narrative summaries, and looking at still photos, I could watch the victim and witnesses talk about what happened and see video of the entire scene. The evidentiary value of body camera recordings cannot be overstated. I was thrilled when, in 2011, the Ada Police Department issued body cameras to all their patrol officers. The Pontotoc County Sheriff's Office expanded the use of body cameras in the summer of 2013. In the fall of 2015, body cameras were issued to all deputies. It became standard practice for all domestic violence cases sent to the District Attorney's Office to include a copy of the body camera video. To their credit, the law enforcement agencies in Pontotoc County were ahead of the curve with regards to body cameras.

Like 911 recordings and jail call recordings, a body camera video's usefulness only matters if it is admitted in court. Unlike 911 recordings and recorded jail calls, body camera videos are a relatively recent tool for law enforcement and prosecutors. Thus, there are not yet many court cases involving evidence or admissibility issues that relate specifically to body camera videos. There likely will be such cases in the future, because the rules of evidence and existing case law provide batterers and their attorneys various means to challenge their admissibility.

One basis for challenging a body camera video is on confrontation grounds. One aspect of body camera videos that is significant is that the camera is being worn by a law enforcement agent. Any instance where a law enforcement agent responds to a domestic disturbance or domestic violence call, any interviews that agent conducts at the scene will be testimonial. The key issue with testimonial statements is that, for them to be admitted, the accused must have the opportunity for cross examination. Whether it is the victim or a third-party witness that was interviewed, the video of the interview is likely not admissible unless that witness appears in court. In that regard, the video of the interview is comparable to a police report or a written witness statement. In a case with an absent victim, this can be a problem. That is one of the reasons why it is important for the victim to be present in court, even if she is uncooperative. Further discussion about having uncooperative victims appear in court can be found in Chapter Four. Provided all the people interviewed or questioned in the video appear in court, the confrontation challenge will fail.

When a body camera video is challenged on confrontation grounds, the objection only applies to testimonial statements. These include any statements that are a response to an officer's questions. Not every statement in a body camera video is part of an interview or a response to a question by law enforcement. It is quite common for the video to catch statements that are not testimonial. I have seen many body camera videos where the batterer, the victim, and children at the scene made spontaneous statements. Often, third party witnesses could be heard talking to each other about what happened. Since most of the people making such statements are not even aware that they are on camera, it is very unlikely that their statements would ever be considered testimonial and therefore should survive a confrontation challenge.

Statements made in a body camera video can also be challenged on hearsay grounds. Like with a confrontation objection, the best way to defeat this challenge is for the person in the video to appear and testify; however, with regards to statements that are not testimonial, it may be possible to overcome the hearsay challenge even if the person who made the statement does not appear. If the statements fall under any of the hearsay exceptions or exclusions, then it can be admitted. For example, spontaneous statements by the victim, a third-party witness, or any children at the scene might constitute an "excited utterance."[103] Background statements by third-party witnesses who are talking to each other about the incident might fit the "present sense impression" exception.[104] Also, any statements by the batterer should fall under the exclusion for statements by a party being used against that party.[105]

The ideal scenario for a prosecutor seeking to admit a body camera video is for all the witnesses in the video to be present in court. When that is the case, another challenge that may be raised is that the video constitutes the needless presentation of cumulative evidence.[106] A cumulative evidence challenge will be based on the argument that, since all the people in the video are present, there is no need to play the video. The fact of the matter is that playing a video of several people making the same statements that those same people have already made in person is cumulative. The key issue with a "cumulative" challenge, however, is whether the cumulative evidence is "needless." So, if all the people in the video testify, then what need is there for the video?

There are two main reasons why the video might still be necessary. First, the video may be necessary for any content outside of verbal statements. This includes any helpful visual imagery. Regardless of which witnesses are present or not, and regardless of what statements are admissible or not, the visual imagery should be admissible. Visual imagery can include people's emotional state, the victim's injuries, and the scene of the assault showing signs of a struggle.

When I have argued against cumulative challenges in the past, I argued that the video was not cumulative in the same way that a photograph is not cumulative even if a witness has already described the photo. For example, in one case I prosecuted, an uncooperative victim testified that her injuries were caused when she walked down the stairs from her second-floor apartment, tripped over the loose bottom step, and was still on the ground where she fell when the police arrived.[107]

The imagery from the video showed that the police officer had to walk about ten steps and go around a corner to get from the bottom of the stairs to the victim's location. The video also showed the victim still lying on the ground when the police arrived. The officer was certainly capable of testifying to those facts, and he did. The video showing how far away the victim was from the stairs, showing her on the ground, and showing her emotional state and demeanor, was more compelling than any verbal description could ever be. Thus, it was not "needless." The visual imagery from the body camera video drove home that the victim's testimony was not accurate.

The other main reason why the body camera video might be necessary is to overcome an uncooperative victim. When a victim is on the stand and has either recanted or is minimizing, the prosecutor bears the burden of proving that her original claim of abuse is true despite her testimony. Prior to body camera video recordings, prosecutors had to overcome uncooperative victim testimony with testimony from third-party witnesses, the victim's original written statement (if provided), testimony from law enforcement, photographs, and so forth.

Prior to body camera videos, it was still possible to succeed in overcoming uncooperative victims when the surrounding evidence was strong enough. In a case where the victim has recanted or minimized and there is body camera video, however, the primary goal is to show the video to the judge or jury. When they see and hear what the officer saw and heard, and get a first-hand look at the victim's condition, emotional state, and demeanor, it is powerful evidence. Also, since the victim's testimony is inconsistent with her statements in the video, the video is not cumulative.

Under certain circumstances, a body camera video might be challenged on the grounds of unlawful search. Part of the training presentation I gave to law enforcement included the importance of viewing the scene of any assault. A full discussion of my law enforcement training materials can be found in Chapter Five. I have seen many body camera videos where the victim gave law enforcement permission to enter the residence to view the scene of the assault. In some cases, the victim not only allowed law enforcement into the residence, but also gave them a "tour" wherein she pointed out where the assault took place, signs of the struggle, and described the assault in detail as the "tour" went along. In one such case, the body camera video was challenged on the basis that, since the batterer did not consent to the search of his home, the video should be suppressed.[108]

This challenge turns on whether the batterer was still at the scene or had left the scene either voluntarily or by being arrested and removed. Also, this challenge only applies to instances where the batterer and the victim share the residence where the assault took place. Per the United States Supreme Court's decision in *Fernandez v. California*, when there is a shared residence, and the victim gives law enforcement consent to search after the batterer has either left or been removed, then the search is lawful because the victim's consent is sufficient.[109]

In the case where I faced this challenge, the batterer and victim shared a residence. Also, the batterer had already been lawfully arrested and removed from the scene when the victim gave consent. The case was settled before trial, so the Court never made a ruling. The Supreme Court's holding in *Fernandez* is clear, however.

Finally, a body camera video might be challenged for containing inadmissible evidence of prior bad acts. In the State of Oklahoma, the first law enforcement responders to interview a domestic violence victim are required to conduct the Lethality Assessment Protocol (LAP). Oklahoma was the first state to institute mandatory LAP. This involves asking the victim a series of questions and taking certain actions depending on the answers.[110]

Several of the questions pertain to the batterer's past behavior. If the body camera video includes the victim's answers to the LAP questions, then the video might contain statements about prior bad acts by the batterer. The video might also contain statements regarding prior bad acts even if the video does not show a LAP. If that is the case, then those statements can be another basis to challenge the video. Evidence of prior bad acts are not admissible to prove the character of a person in order to show action in conformity therewith.[111]

In simpler terms, it is generally not permissible to try and prove that a person is guilty of a present crime or bad act because that person has a history of doing bad things. There are other specific purposes for which evidence of prior bad acts is admissible, however, provided that the prosecutor filed a written notice of intent to admit such evidence prior to trial.[112] Among those purposes are to show intent and lack of mistake or accident. These two purposes are important in a domestic violence case with an uncooperative victim. If the body camera video contains the LAP, and the victim's answers refer to past acts of aggression or abuse, then those statements may be admissible if the victim either recants or tries to minimize.

It is common for uncooperative victims to say that the incident was an accident, or that the batterer did not intend to strike them or commit the assault. After a victim testifies that the incident was unintentional or accidental, the door should be open to admit the statements from the video about prior bad acts to show intent or the lack of mistake or accident.

Body camera videos offer additional benefits beyond their evidentiary value in the courtroom. There are two other significant benefits. The first pertains to witness preparation. Witnesses are often called to testify months after the incident took place. Prior to a witness taking the stand, it is common practice for the prosecutor to go over their anticipated testimony. Part of preparing the witness to testify involves refreshing their memory about the case. This is permitted because memories can fade over time.

Prior to body camera videos, this involved providing the witness with a copy of any written statement they had provided so they could read it and refresh their recollection. Body camera videos can serve the same purpose. The prosecutor can show the witness the portion of the video containing that witness' interview. Thus, instead of relying solely on what they wrote, the witness can watch their entire interview. The combination of seeing the entire interview and the imagery, such as the scene, the clothes they were wearing, and so forth, will prepare the witness to testify accurately much more effectively than a written statement.

When the witness is the officer that was wearing the camera, the video is also important for witness preparation. Writing reports about incidents is standard practice for law enforcement; however, the practical reality for people working in law enforcement is that the reports cannot always be written immediately. It is common for an officer to respond to multiple calls or incidents before there is any chance to write the reports. Also, there is no way that any police report can contain every single detail about an incident.

When someone from law enforcement is cross examined, they are likely going to face questions intended to raise doubts about their ability to remember or the accuracy of their report. This may include questions about how long after the incident they wrote the report, how sure they are that the report is complete, and if they are relying on their report for their testimony. If the incident was the first of four or five calls that the officer responded to without any time in between, then the report may not have been written for several hours, or possibly not until the following day. Any time a police officer must testify that they were not able to write the report until the day after the incident, that officer is open to questions about how accurate the report is. If that officer is relying on the report for their testimony, then any doubts raised about the report carry over to their testimony.

A body camera video eliminates all of that. The officer needs only review the body camera video prior to testifying. The officer can also review the body camera video while writing the report, which can mitigate any issues related to the passage of time. Once the officer testifies that their entire response to the incident was captured on video, and that they reviewed the video before taking the stand, any issues about the police report or the officer's ability to remember should be cured.

What Are You Doing with This?

The second additional benefit of body camera videos is that they reduce the likelihood that a case will go to trial at all. A body camera video can both strengthen a prosecutor's case and help the prosecutor prepare for trial more effectively. Together, those benefits are a compelling reason for any batterer to settle their case instead of demanding their day in court, even if the victim is uncooperative.

I have prosecuted numerous domestic violence cases with uncooperative victims where a body camera video helped me succeed in resolving a case prior to trial. In one such case, the video begins with a police officer walking towards the back door or side door to a residence.[113] A ramp led to the door. The victim was standing on the ramp, facing away from the house, leaning against the railing, and crying.

As the officer approached the bottom of the ramp the victim made a spontaneous statement that she and her boyfriend had been fighting and that he had been drinking. The officer then asked her if she was okay and initiated an interview. At that point, it was already clear that she was in extreme distress. While she could talk to the officer, it was a struggle for her because she was so upset that she had to try and speak between sobs and was very choked up.

Shortly after the interview started, the officer interrupted one of her answers and asked, "What are you doing with this?" To which she replied, "Because he was hitting me." The officer then took something from her and placed it on the ground at the bottom of the ramp. She had been holding a large kitchen knife. After the interview resumed, the victim turned towards the officer, which brought her face into better light. There was a knot on her forehead approximately the size of a golf ball. The victim explained that the knot was from the batterer head-butting her.

All that imagery and all those statements occurred in the first two minutes of the video. The victim's initial spontaneous statement, provided she was present in court, would likely have been admissible as an "excited utterance" since it was not a response to a question. The fact that she was holding a knife was strong circumstantial evidence that she was assaulted since the knife was evidence that she was in fear for her own safety. The imagery of the knife was certainly admissible. Her emotional state, demeanor, and difficulty speaking were also admissible and was strong evidence that she had recently been through a traumatic experience. Also, the imagery of the large knot in the middle of her forehead was admissible, and consistent with her description of the assault.

The first two minutes of the video contained enough evidence to successfully prosecute the case without a trial. That was important because three minutes into the video the victim asked the officers, "What if I don't want y'all to arrest him?" In some instances, domestic violence victims are uncooperative from the moment law enforcement arrives. In other instances, such as in this video, a victim might be cooperative while they are in fear for their immediate safety only to become less cooperative or uncooperative once there is no more immediate danger. In either instance, the likelihood that law enforcement will ever receive a written statement from the victim or receive permission to take still photographs of any injuries is low. Prior to body camera videos, this would be a serious problem.

In the previous section, I discussed how, prior to body-camera videos, testimony from an uncooperative victim had to be overcome with other evidence such as a written statement or still photographs. That was not possible if the victim never provided a written statement or never gave law enforcement consent to photograph her injuries. In such circumstances, success required third party witnesses or evidence such as helpful jail calls. In many cases, neither of those were available. With body camera videos, the game has changed. An uncooperative victim can refuse to provide a statement and refuse to be photographed, but there will still be a recorded statement, including her appearance, emotional state, demeanor, and imagery of any visible injuries.

Without the first two minutes of that video, I am not sure that I could have successfully prosecuted that batterer. There were no third-party witnesses, and the victim never provided a written statement. Since she started showing clear signs of not cooperating about three minutes after the police arrived, it is less likely that she would have consented to photographs of her injuries. Had that case gone to trial, she probably would have recanted on the stand.

Without a body camera video, I would have had less evidence with which to challenge her testimony. The responding officers could have testified about her emotional state, her visible injuries, the kitchen knife, and likely her spontaneous statement. The knife itself could have been brought in to corroborate some of the officers' testimony and reinforce the notion that it was unlikely that a person would be outside of their house with a kitchen knife because they tripped and fell and hit their head. There is no way to know what would have happened had that case gone to trial without the video, but it would have been a tough case to win, because I was armed with that video, however, that batterer had no hope of winning. The video changed the game.

What's Good for the Goose....

Technology is not the only answer to overcoming uncooperative victims or the only way to have the facts on your side. The usefulness of facts can be affected by the order in which they are presented. There are two helpful approaches a prosecutor can use to alter the order in which facts are presented. These two approaches are based on the concepts of primacy, recency, and preemption.

These concepts mean that the first thing the judge or jury hears (primacy) and last thing the judge or jury hears (recency) will be more salient than the material presented in between. With this in mind, it is better for a prosecutor to address harmful issues and frame them first rather than let the other party be the first to raise those issues (preemption).

Preemption includes attacking a harmful issue or adverse testimony in advance. In my experience, the two helpful approaches to applying these concepts are the way an entire case is presented, and the way individual parts of a case are presented.

With regard to the entire case, applying these concepts starts with the opening statement. In a domestic violence trial with an uncooperative victim, the judge or jury, at some point, is going to find out that the victim does not support the prosecution.

They will either find out through her testimony or her absence. Thus, the prosecutor has two options. The prosecutor can either break the news to the judge or jury first (preemption) or let the other side do it. Whichever side breaks that news first will be able to frame the issue and choose the context.

In my opinion, it is better if the prosecutor breaks the news in the opening statement. This is where primacy enters the picture. If the prosecutor does not raise the issue during opening statements, then the other side certainly will, which means the other side can frame the issue and choose the context. It almost goes without saying that, in any domestic violence trial with an uncooperative victim, the victim's testimony or absence will be a point of emphasis for the defense. If the defense can raise that issue and frame it, then, due to primacy, that issue will be a cloud over the prosecution's case for the entire trial. Everything else presented to the judge or jury will be viewed through that lens. Also, the defense can point out the fact that the prosecution neglected to mention it. That is a bad place for the prosecutor to be.

Another approach to utilizing primacy and recency with regard to the entire case is witness order. Typically, the attorney trying the case has discretion over the order in which the witnesses are called. An uncooperative victim does not have to testify first. In my opinion, an uncooperative victim should never testify first. If she is the first witness, then the first testimony the judge or jury will hear is the victim recanting or minimizing. That testimony will be a cloud over the rest of the prosecution's case.

Instead, call the domestic violence expert first. After preempting that the victim is uncooperative during opening statements and framing that issue, let the expert explain why victims recant, minimize, and often oppose the prosecution. That way, the expert's testimony can be a cloud over the other side's case for the rest of the trial.

When the uncooperative victim does eventually take the stand, the judge or jury will view her testimony through that lens. The difference between applying preemption and primacy and not applying them is tremendous.

As noted above, applying the primacy, recency, and preemption concepts, one goal for the prosecutor is to have the uncooperative victim's testimony buried in the middle of their case.

Another goal is to take steps to soften the blow. Thus, the second witness should be one that brings strong evidence of guilt and should not be the victim. This might be a good place to have the investigating officer testify about the victim's appearance, emotional state, demeanor, or any visible injuries and admit any photographs of the victim's injuries or any signs of struggle at the scene. If there is a body-camera video, then the officer wearing the camera will likely need to testify before the victim and lay the proper foundation so that the video can be used when the victim testifies. Another option is for the second witness to be the person to introduce the 911 call if the call recording is helpful.

If the victim sought or received any medical treatment for her injuries, or went to the emergency room, then it might be helpful for the second witness to be the paramedic, nurse, or doctor that treated the victim. If there was a third-party witness to the assault, then I would definitely call that person as the second witness. In cases where several of these options are available, I would call all of them to testify before the victim. The goal is to convince the judge or jury that the batterer is guilty before the victim testifies and preempt the victim's testimony. The closer the prosecutor can get to that goal, then the harder it is for the victim's testimony to change the judge or jury's mind.

Also, the closer the prosecutor gets to that goal, the more likely it becomes that the victim's testimony will validate the expert's testimony. In my opinion, if the judge or jury is already convinced, or nearly convinced, that the batterer is guilty when they hear the victim recant or try to minimize, then they are more likely to conclude that the victim is simply behaving the way that the expert said she would behave. When the judge or jury reaches that conclusion, they have no reason to doubt the batterer's guilt.

Recency plays a role in witness order as well. Thus, in my opinion, an uncooperative victim should not be the last witness. I would not want to conclude my case with a witness that testified that there was no assault or that the incident was an accident. If an uncooperative victim is the last prosecution witness, then the last thing the judge or jury hears from the prosecution's case is the defense cross examining the victim and emphasizing her recanting or minimizing testimony. That amounts to the defense usurping the recency concept, which is bad.

The list of examples for witnesses to call after the victim is like the list of witnesses to call in between the expert and the victim; however, each case is unique. Some cases have more witnesses than others. Occasionally, there are not many witnesses to call other than the victim, the expert, and the investigating officer. If that is the case then the expert should still testify first, and the officer may need to testify before the victim when there is a body camera video. That leaves the victim as the last witness. While that is not ideal, it is the best outcome under those circumstances.

Under more ideal circumstances, I prefer to conclude my case with helpful jail call recordings. In my opinion, the most effective way to apply the recency concept is for the judge or jury to hear incriminating statements from the batterer at the end of the prosecution's case. Saving the jail calls for last has the added benefit of preventing the defense from usurping the recency concept. If the jail call recordings are brought in at the end, then the witness is likely going to be a jail employee that manages the jail recording system, such as the jail administrator, office manager, or someone working in a similar capacity. It is unlikely that person has any knowledge of the case. Instead, they merely located the recordings in the system and put them on a disk, and so that is all they will testify to. Thus, there are no strong points for the defense to make on cross examination.

Primacy, recency, and preemption can also be utilized when the victim is absent. If the victim refuses to appear at the trial, the prosecutor should preempt that during opening statements. The expert witness should still testify first to explain the victim's behavior. That way, the judge or jury can view the rest of the state's case through that lens. There is obviously no need to arrange the witness order to bury the victim's testimony in the middle or to prevent the victim from testifying last, so that aspect of witness order is moot. When possible, I would still conclude the case with helpful jail call recordings.

Applying these concepts to individual parts of a case also centers on topic order or question order used with a witness. This approach does not apply to witnesses whose testimony is narrow in scope. For example, witnesses called to admit a 911 recording or jail call recordings should only testify about that one topic. Other witnesses, however, such as the investigating officer or an uncooperative victim, typically testify about several topics and face several lines of questioning.

Applying primacy, recency, and preemption is an effective way to decide how to put the topics in order. The most helpful or persuasive topics, or lines of questioning, should be at the start and the end of the examination. For example, if there are photographs of the victim's injuries that depict severe bruising, lacerations, or swelling, then when the investigating officer testifies, use the first line of questioning to admit those photographs.

Once they are admitted, the rest of the officer's testimony will likely be viewed through that lens. Also, any testimony the officer has about the victim being uncoopera-tive should be brought up during questioning to preempt those details but should be buried in the middle of the officer's testimony.

For example, if the victim refused to provide a written statement or refused to give law enforcement consent to enter the residence, the officer will testify to that at some point. It is better for those details to emerge in the middle of the direct examination while the judge or jury are likely still thinking about the victim's injuries than at the end of the defense's cross examination. In cases where the batterer fled the scene before law enforcement arrived, that can be a good topic to put at the end of the officer's testimony.

With regards to uncooperative victims, applying primacy, recency, and preemption to determine topic order or question order can also be a way to overcome the harmful testimony. If a prosecutor calls an uncooperative victim to the stand and asks her to describe the incident, then the victim is going to recant or minimize. Do not lead with that. There is no requirement that the victim's testimony be elicited in chronological order.

Instead, devote the first substantive line of questioning to a detail or topic that is difficult to explain away. For example, if the case involved the victim locking herself in a room and the batterer forcing entry into that room, then start with that detail. If there are photographs of the damaged door or doorframe, then those photographs should be admitted before the victim is called to the stand. Show the victim the photograph and ask her how it happened.

It would be difficult for a victim to explain how it happened and then reconcile her explanation with her recanting or minimizing testimony. Another example is the case discussed in the previous section. If that case had gone to trial and that victim was on the stand, my first line of questioning would have been about the knife she was holding. I would open my examination by asking her to explain why she was standing outside on the ramp holding that large kitchen knife when the police arrived. In my opinion, it would have been hard for her to explain the knife, then later testify that she was not assaulted. I would have concluded my examination on a similarly strong point, such as her statement to the responding officers that the knot on her head was from a headbutt.

At some point, either during the direct examination or on cross examination, an uncooperative victim will have the opportunity to give her recanting or minimizing testimony about the incident. Since it is going to come out anyway, the best approach is to bring it out during the direct examination and bury it in the middle. Even if it is buried in the middle, there is still no requirement that it be elicited in chronological order. In some cases, it may not matter if the victim testifies about the incident in chronological order. In other cases, it may be helpful to use a different approach. In cases where the victim ended up in the emergency room or the hospital, I prefer starting from the end and working backwards. This approach entails asking the victim to explain the nature of her injuries, why she went to the hospital or emergency room, how she got there, and so forth before inquiring about how the incident started or how the incident unfolded. In my opinion, this approach is an effective way to elicit the recanting or minimizing testimony because the more topics and questions that the victim must answer before she has an opportunity to testify about the incident, the harder it will be for her to recant or minimize in a consistent manner.

Testifying in court is often a traumatic experience for domestic-violence victims. Testifying about the abuse involves reliving it. The approaches I have just discussed can amplify that because, in addition to reliving the abuse, these approaches can effectively box the victim in such that she might not be able to avoid admitting things that she does not want to admit.

I will not sugarcoat it. These approaches can be harsh. I prefer not to use any of them, and I endeavored not to. One choice is to avoid putting victims on the stand at all. Further discussion of this topic can be found in Chapter Four.

One final point about having the facts on your side pertains to a defense argument I have encountered on several occasions. In my experience, it is common for the defense to try and put the victim on trial in a domestic violence case. To that end, the defense may try to portray the victim as the problem in the relationship.

This argument typically involves two parts. First, that the victim is the instigator of arguments or fights. Second, that if the batterer was abusive, then why is the victim still in the relationship? Anyone that is well versed in the dynamics of abusive relationships likely knows the answer to the second part of that argument. Most jurors, however, are not likely to be well versed in the dynamics of domestic violence, so that part of the argument might be persuasive.

The most effective response to this argument is to turn the tables by arguing that, if she is such a bad person, then why is he still in the relationship?

CHAPTER FOUR

Have the Victim on Your Side

There are two ways for domestic violence prosecutors to have the victim on their side. The first is for the victim to literally be on their side, which means that the victim is cooperative and supports the prosecution. Obviously, when the victim is cooperative, any problems or difficulties arising from an uncooperative victim are not present.

In some cases, the victim is cooperative from the start. In other cases, a victim may be uncooperative initially but then become cooperative. In my experience, this can be the result of addressing the victim's concerns, which I discussed near the end of Chapter One. I have prosecuted many cases where the victim was uncooperative because she was expecting the batterer to serve time in jail or prison and lose his job, and she was opposed to that because she wanted him to keep his job and get help. In some of those cases, after I informed the victim that I was willing to offer the batterer probation and counseling, the victim agreed to cooperate if the batterer rejected the offer. Most of those cases were misdemeanor cases.

The second way is for the victim to be on the prosecution's side in a figurative sense. This chapter focuses on how the prosecutor can get the victim on their side even when she is uncooperative, and why it is important for her to be present in court even when she does not want to.

This chapter will not contain references to scientific studies, scientific research, or statistics on the issues discussed. That is by design. The contents herein are my views based on my experiences as a domestic violence prosecutor and the discussions of these issues that I have had with other people working in the field, such as law enforcement personnel, victim services providers, and other domestic violence prosecutors.

It Only Matters That She's There

If you have the knowledge on your side, the law on your side, and the facts on your side, then having an uncooperative victim on your side means having her present in the courthouse. While she may not be supportive, she is on your side in a figurative sense because her mere presence is important.

The central theme of this book is how to succeed in domestic violence cases with uncooperative victims. The concepts, approaches, and strategies discussed in this book, when fully utilized, should allow a prosecutor to succeed whether the victim is cooperative or not because the case is not built around the victim's cooperation.

Instead, the prosecutor's case is structured around other evidence so that the prosecutor does not have to depend on the victim's cooperation. This is often referred to as evidence-based prosecution.

Even when employing evidence-based prosecution, however, succeeding in court is difficult, and, in some cases, impossible, when the victim is absent entirely. Some of the reasons for that were discussed in the previous chapter. In my experience, to be consistently successful prosecuting domestic violence cases, the victims need to be present in court. A phrase I often used was that "it doesn't matter what she says, it only matters that she's there."

A core component of evidence-based prosecution is a no-drop policy. That means the prosecutor will not dismiss or decline to file a domestic violence case at the victim's request. The District Attorney's Office is not obligated to file charges in every case received, but rather exercises discretion over which cases merit criminal charges and which cases do not.

A no-drop policy covers requests by victims to drop the charges at the outset of the case, such as those found in yellow pad letters, requests made during victim meetings, and requests made later in the process because the victim does not want to appear in court.

The last of those is particularly significant. A no-drop policy is not compatible with a policy where the victim decides whether to appear in court. As I mentioned earlier, successfully prosecuting cases with absent victims is difficult because some evidence cannot be admitted when the victim is absent.

Cases with absent victims will succeed at a much lower rate than cases with uncooperative victims that are present. The core concept behind evidence-based prosecution is being able to succeed without depending on the victim's cooperation. If the uncooperative victim gets to decide whether to appear, then the prosecutor's success is dependent on the victim's choice instead of the evidence. The question that naturally follows is what a prosecutor should do when a victim refuses to appear. This is not an easy question. There are various factors to consider, and some of them are opposing factors.

The answer to that question, in my opinion, needs to be a consistent policy. Either victims will be compelled to appear or not. In my experience, it will not work to be selective about when to compel victims to appear. For example, if victims are compelled to appear only in felony cases, then misdemeanor cases will suffer. Recall that in misdemeanor cases, the batterers are less likely to spend significant time in jail while the case is pending. Thus, recorded jail calls are less likely to exist, and any intimidation efforts will likely happen in private since the batterer will have direct access to the victim. Such a selective approach encourages misdemeanor batterers to tamper with their victims with little fear of consequence since evidence to support an intimidation action or a Forfeiture by Wrong-doing action will be absent.

Prosecutors applying this selective approach will likely find themselves handling more misdemeanor cases with absent victims. An increase in cases with absent victims will cause a decrease in successful prosecution rates. That is not a good place for the prosecutor to be. Also, I use the term "successful prosecution rate" instead of "conviction rate" deliberately. I define the term "successful prosecution" to mean any outcome where the case can serve as a valid enhancer if the batterer reoffends and the batterer is ordered to complete a domestic violence program, such as a Batterer's Intervention Program, or BIP. In some cases, these goals can be achieved even if the batterer is not convicted.

It is important for me to be clear on what I mean by compelling victims to appear. Compelling victims to appear means taking all available steps to get them properly served with subpoenas and then enforcing the subpoenas.

Enforcing subpoenas means pursuing contempt of court actions and arrest warrants for victims who disobey subpoenas. If there are no consequences for victims who disobey subpoenas, then there is no reason for them to feel compelled to appear. Also, I used the term "better policy" in the previous paragraph for a reason. There is nothing "good" about compelling victims to appear against their will. I consider it a necessary evil. I support that approach because I believe it is better than the alternative.

There is no reason to sugar coat anything. Pursuing contempt charges or warrants for domestic violence victims that refuse to appear in court is a harsh policy. Domestic violence victims typically have good reason to avoid the witness stand. When she takes the witness stand, there are consequences. Some of these are certain and some are possibilities.

The certain consequences include the traumatic effects of re-living the assault (or assaults), facing the batterer in court, and the inherent strain involved when she must answer personal and uncomfortable questions in front of strangers.

The possible consequences include backlash from the batterer's family (both before and after appearing in court), and the threat of retribution or retaliation. In many cases where the victim testifies to the assault or abuse, the threat of retaliation is real.

Not every uncooperative victim recants or minimizes. The first three chapters of this book focus heavily on uncooperative victims that recant, minimize, or are absent. I have, however, prosecuted cases where the victim did not support the prosecution, did not want to testify, but ultimately testified consistently with her original claim of abuse. Unfortunately, in doing so, they often admit to incriminating facts and details even if they did not want to, testimony that can trigger the threat of retaliation.

Not everyone who works in a field related to domestic violence agrees that compelling victims to appear is the better approach. During my time in Ada, I met people whose views were like my own, and I met people who held opposing views. I have had numerous discussions about this issue. I have also read articles and other source material on this. It's a point in question I take very seriously. I can understand people's resistance to issuing an arrest warrant for a domestic violence victim.

There is an alternative approach that does not involve contempt of court actions or warrants for victims who disobey subpoenas. One of the conditions for receiving grant funds from the Department of Justice Office on Violence Against Women (OVW) is that the recipient may not use the grant funds to support activities that compromise victim safety, including penalizing victims who refuse to testify.[114]

The alternative approach, as I see it, is to try and convince more victims to cooperate and appear voluntarily, rely on other evidence to succeed in cases where the victim is absent, and accept any acquittals or dismissals as a necessary sacrifice to protect victims from facing the consequences of testifying if they do not want to testify. I have also encountered the argument that compelling victims to appear might discourage women from reporting instances of abuse to the authorities.

Considering how testifying is typically traumatic for domestic violence victims, and considering some of the other consequences they might face, how is it better to compel them to appear if they do not want to?

That is a fair question. I can understand anyone asking how, in good conscience, I could compel a victim to go through such an ordeal or seek to have them arrested if they refused. The answer is that, while compelling victims to appear in court is harsh, the alternative is worse. The problem I have with the alternative approach, and the primary reason I do not agree with it, is that the alternative approach shows no consideration for anything beyond protecting the victim from the trauma or consequences of testifying.

There are other sources of trauma and danger besides the witness stand. It is easy to support the alternative approach when the only consideration is the benefit, and no consideration is given to the cost. The alternative approach, in my opinion, loses its luster when you see how it does far more harm than good for victims. Allowing victims to refuse to appear exposes victims to greater trauma and greater danger than compelling them to appear.

You may have noticed that I have framed this issue to be about compelling victims to appear, as opposed to compelling victims to testify. I did that deliberately because there is a difference between appearing in court and taking the witness stand. This is an important distinction. If a victim appears in court but does not take the witness stand, there are far less consequences for her.

The consequences though, are not eliminated entirely. Even if the victim never takes the stand, there are often backlash and intimidation efforts made prior to the court date. Also, when victims are in the waiting area and do not know if they will testify or not, that experience is typically unpleasant. The alternative approach, in my opinion, rests on an assumption that victims who are compelled to appear will be asked to testify. That is a false assumption. In my experience, the victim's presence significantly reduces the likelihood that the hearing or trial will proceed. It may seem counterintuitive, but compelling victims to appear is an effective way to reduce the need for victims to testify.

In my experience, domestic violence cases fall into three categories. The first consists of batterers that show no interest in contesting the case. They take a deal and go on. In this case, witnesses are typically not subpoenaed at all, so her need to appear is a moot point.

The second category consists of batterers who contest the charges with an absentee victim defense. For these cases, the victim's appearance is typically the pivotal issue.

The third category consists of the batterers that contest the charges on the merits. This includes batterers who claim self-defense and whose strategy includes putting the victim on trial.

During my last few years working in Ada, when I was using all the strategies and approaches discussed in this book, the first group was the largest. The law enforcement personnel I worked with were well trained and consistently made domestic violence cases a point of emphasis. Thus, I typically received strong cases, most of which were bolstered by body camera videos. That deterred a lot of batterers from demanding their day in court.

The second category was the next largest. Batterers in this situation were the focus of our mandatory victim appearance policy. Typically, these batterers tried to keep the victim from appearing and were waiting to see if she showed up. When the victim agreed to appear, the batterer was often motivated to take a deal and resolve the case.

If the victim did not plan to appear then the batterer typically insisted that they were innocent and demanded their day in court.

Batterers in the third category were, by far, the most likely to take their case to trial regardless of whether the victim appeared.

With regards to the second category, here was how I typically identified those cases. I would meet with the defendant and the attorney (if he had one) before the preliminary hearing or the misdemeanor trial and tell the defendant point blank that his only leverage with me was to help protect the victim from having to testify. I could only use that approach if the victim was present. The batterer rarely cared if she had to testify, but when I told him that, if I must call her to the stand, all deals and negotiations are off. This typically got his attention.

In many cases, this was when I found out if the batterer fit the second category or the third category. In most cases, it turned out to be the second category, and the case was resolved without the victim ever taking the stand. The victim's presence gave me leverage in plea negotiations, and I used that leverage to resolve cases without calling the victim to the stand. For the few cases where the batterer chose to proceed with the hearing or trial, I made sure the victim would be present and ready to proceed.

With absent victims, however, very few cases are settled. Most of the category two cases will become category three. Also, a prosecutor using the alternative approach has no basis for seeking a continuance if the victim fails to appear since the victim would likely be absent for any future setting as well. Under my approach, if a victim was absent and there had been no previous continuances, I could seek a continuance and assure the court that we would compel the victim to appear.

Sometimes it is still possible to succeed with an absent victim. Cases with helpful jail call recordings, 911 recordings, or reliable third-party witnesses can be strong enough to overcome her absence. Cases where there is evidence of witness tampering or evidence supporting a Forfeiture by Wrongdoing action might also succeed with an absent victim.

But proceeding based exclusively on other evidence or Forfeiture by Wrongdoing actions is not any kind of panacea. Successfully prosecuting domestic violence cases with absent victims is more the exception than the rule. As I stated before, many batterers, particularly in misdemeanor cases, do not stay in jail very long and thus stay off the phone. Much of the witness intimidation or tampering by batterers takes place behind closed doors. Also, in cases where the victim is intimidated or tampered with by the batterer's friends or family, there is rarely any way to prove it without the victim.

The batterer's friends or family certainly will not come forward and admit it. With regards to cases where incriminating jail calls were made, the participants usually make statements that establish who is talking, but not always. I have listened to jail calls where nobody identifies anyone by name or makes any comments that help identify the participants. In such cases, without the victim, it would be difficult to identify the participants and admit the calls. Also, any written statement provided by the victim will be inadmissible under *Hammon v. Indiana* if the victim is absent.

Any verbal statement in a body camera video will likely be inadmissible as well. Photographs or video imagery of the victim's injuries are less helpful if there is no evidence to explain what caused the injuries. In my experience, with regards to misdemeanor cases, it is rare for the victim to receive any medical treatment, which eliminates any hope of calling an EMT, nurse, or doctor as a witness. Also, most domestic violence incidents happen in a private setting. In my experience, it is rare for a third party to witness the assault. In the end, the successful prosecution rate for domestic violence cases with absent victims will always be low, especially in misdemeanor cases.

When the alternative approach is being used, and victims are not compelled to appear, the result will be a lot of absent victims. Under the alternative approach, the idea is that improved efforts to connect victims with victim services providers, such as counselors and advocates, and improved communication between the prosecutor and the victim will lead to more victims voluntarily appearing.

This approach lacks consideration for the batterer's influence over the victim's decision to appear. Batterers have power and control in the relationship. They often use it to discourage their victims from receiving services or communicating with the prosecutor. This is because they know that their chances of beating the case are much higher if the victim is absent.

Batterers typically do not want their victims communicating with people, such as advocates or counselors, that might empower them or encourage them to cooperate. Advocates, counselors, and prosecutors have little hope of matching the batterer's influence over the victim. Thus, despite any such efforts, victims who do not want to testify are typically not going to appear in court if they do not have to. If they know they will not be penalized, then they know that they don't have to appear.

This leads to reduced successful prosecution rates in two ways. The first, which is described in the previous paragraph, is that absent victims weaken the prosecutors' cases and lead to more dismissals and acquittals. The second is that the alternative approach increases the size of category two and decreases the size of category one.

When the District Attorney's policy is that victims will not be penalized for refusing to appear, victims will know it. The batterers, or people working on their behalf, will see to it. Also, the local defense bar will be aware of it. In cases where the batterer has an attorney and the victim does not want to appear, the attorney will likely explain to the client that the victim will not be penalized for refusing to appear. The batterer will then "explain" it to the victim. The attorney might also explain it to the victim directly.

Regardless of any ethical questions this action may raise, it will happen. Also, the defense attorney might try to take advantage of the grant conditions to help keep the victim from appearing. Although I was not subject to the OVW grant conditions while working in Ada, attorneys from out of the area were not always aware of that.

In one case, a defense attorney explicitly told me that the victim was not going to appear and that I could not compel her to because I would lose my funding. For offices relying on OVW grant funds, his threat would be valid. That a defense attorney can use the OVW grant condition as a tool to help a batterer beat his charges further illustrates that the grant condition is not a good approach to protecting victims.

When the policy that victims will not be penalized is combined with the fact that cases are harder to prove with absent victims, what incentive is there for the batterer to take a deal? Outside of the few cases with strong evidence separate from the victim's testimony, there is no incentive. Thus, batterers who would otherwise fall into category one migrate into category two. Then, when their victims are absent, they migrate into category three, and successful prosecution rates plummet.[115]

Why do successful prosecution rates matter? Also, why is the successful prosecution rate in misdemeanor cases important? Is it just about prosecutors having more notches on their gun belts? No. Higher successful prosecution rates have far-reaching effects on increasing victim safety. Low prosecution rates, particularly in misdemeanor cases, have far-reaching effects on reducing victim safety.

To explain this, I need to discuss some of the dynamics of domestic violence and abusive relationships. In legal parlance, I need to lay some foundation. There is a strong correlation between uncooperative victims and victims who remain in the relationship with their batterer. I can probably count on one hand the number of cases I have prosecuted where a victim left the relationship and still refused to cooperate. When a victim is uncooperative or does not want to appear, that victim is almost always still in the relationship with the batterer.

So, why does it matter that uncooperative victims are typically still in the relationship? The answer pertains to one of the core dynamics of abusive relationships, which is the batterer's power and control over the victim. Other common aspects, such as isolation, dependence, attacks on the victim's self-esteem, and so forth, facilitate the batterer's power and control over the victim. When they try to keep their victims from appearing in court, they are exercising their power and control. If a batterer succeeds in keeping his victim from appearing, then his power and control is reinforced. If the victim appears against the batterer's wishes, then his power and control is diminished.

Also, as I have stated, batterers frequently try to intimidate, manipulate, and tamper with their victims. These activities usually take place while the case is pending. If the batterer is out of jail, then it is a safe bet that these activities are going on behind closed doors.

When the batterer is in jail, these activities often show up in jail call recordings. In some cases, third parties, such as the batterer's friends or family, may also be involved.

In many cases, acts of manipulation and tampering take place before the assault. Batterers often try to isolate their victims. This means severing the victim's connection to any support system, such as their close friends and family. In some cases, this includes geographic isolation where the batterer convinces the victim to move away to a new city or town and away from any friends or family.

Batterers also try to create dependency. This typically involves assuming control over the finances by having the home, the bank accounts, and bills in his name, and by being the primary income earner.

The isolation and dependency often create a situation where, if the batterer is jailed or successfully prosecuted, the victim will end up in a precarious situation. I have prosecuted many cases where the victim's primary reason for trying to drop the charges was the fear that, if the case persisted, she would be left homeless and broke. In those cases, the batterer effectively tampered with the victim before the fact.

The case discussed at the end of Chapter One, which included the body camera video discussed in Chapter Three, is a good example. Recall that, in that case, the victim transitioned from cooperative to uncooperative in about three minutes after the police arrived. Also, recall that she feared what would happen to herself and her children if he was prosecuted. She went from holding a knife for protection to not wanting the batterer arrested, and the batterer never said a word to her. He did not have to.

The reason she switched from cooperative to uncooperative so quickly was that, once she was safe, it dawned on her that he was the only income earner, their house belonged to his father, and she had children to take care of. She also knew that he was already on probation. She knew that if he was prosecuted, she and her children would be homeless and broke.

There was no intimidation or Forfeiture by Wrongdoing behavior after the arrest that we could find. There were no jail calls. She never visited him at the jail, but the intimidation still happened and led to her not cooperating. It was all done before he gave her that knot on her forehead. He did not need to say anything to get her to try and drop the charges because he set it up in advance. Her predicament was not uncommon.

With the tampering and intimidation that often happen before and after the assault, a victim's refusal to cooperate is rarely an independent decision. Instead, her decision reflects the batterer's power and control in the relationship. If the prosecutor's policy is to let domestic violence victims choose whether to appear, then, in many cases, it is the batterer who is making the decision. Batterers and their attorneys know, just as I do, that their chances of beating the case are much higher if the victim is absent. If the prosecutor employs a policy that hands the batterers what they want, the result is batterers essentially signing their own dismissals. When it comes to protecting victims from additional trauma and promoting victim safety, that is not the answer.

Another reason why it matters that uncooperative victims are typically still in the relationship is what happens after the batterer's case is declined or dismissed.

For there to be a case in the first place, a report of abuse must have been made to law enforcement with sufficient evidence for charges to be filed. Very few domestic violence cases are filed without, at the very least, an initial claim of abuse by the victim. Thus, when a domestic violence case is declined or dismissed because the victim refused to appear, it is likely she was tampered with by the batterer in some way and is still in the relationship.

That is not a safe situation. That victim is most likely going to suffer additional abuse and trauma. Also, any possibility that the victim might have faced retaliation for testifying, is replaced by the near certainty that she will face retaliation for reporting the abuse in the first place. The alternative approach does not only trap victims in abusive relationships. It also gives the batterer another reason to be abusive.

Furthermore, when the progressive nature of abusive relationships is factored in, it is likely that subsequent acts of abuse will increase in frequency and severity. This means not just more abuse, but worse abuse. Abusive intimate partner relationships often escalate over time if there is no intervention.[116]

This is where the focus on misdemeanor cases comes in. Misdemeanor cases are often first offenses for the batterer or involve relatively minor incidents.[117] When a misdemeanor case is successfully prosecuted, that intervention carries the potential to prevent any escalation, which is good for the victim's safety. When a misdemeanor case is unsuccessfully prosecuted, the opposite is true. When the alternative approach is used, and the successful prosecution rate for misdemeanor cases plummets, many opportunities for intervention are lost and many abusive relationships can escalate.

Also, after the case is dismissed or declined, the batterer can, and will, show his victim the futility in reporting abuse. There is no greater deterrent preventing victims from reporting abuse than situations where a victim reports abuse, nothing comes of it, and that victim ends up trapped deeper in the abusive relationship.

What reason is there for that victim to report abuse ever again? None. It is true that, when the alternative approach is used, such a victim is spared the trauma and consequences of testifying; however, when the abuse starts up again and gets worse, I doubt it is any consolation. The alternative approach protects victims from testifying only to leave them trapped deeper in abusive relationships with less reason to report subsequent acts of abuse. When you factor in how the alternative approach causes successful prosecution rates to plummet, that means more victims trapped in abusive relationships, more victims facing subsequent abuse, and more victims with less reason to report abuse.

Under the alternative approach, victims are being pulled from the frying pan and thrown right into the fire. The only way to prevent that outcome is to compel victims to appear in court, even if it means contempt of court actions or arrest warrants.

Throwing more victims into the fire is not the only consequence of low successful prosecution rates. Another is that low successful prosecution rates discourage law enforcement from devoting the time and resources necessary to support an evidence-based approach. This is not a criticism of law enforcement. I want to be clear on that. Nor is it a suggestion that law enforcement personnel are tolerant of domestic violence. In my experience, the opposite is true.

For an evidence-based approach to work, however, law enforcement personnel in the field must be on board. That means participating in domestic violence training and applying what they learn. That also means devoting more time and resources to the investigations. Law enforcement personnel are typically busy and typically carry large caseloads. They must prioritize how they spend their time and resources. It is difficult to convince law enforcement to make domestic violence a priority if many of the cases they submit are declined or dismissed. If successful prosecution rates are low due to cases being declined or dismissed, it will likely lead to disillusionment and frustration for law enforcement.

Again, this is not a criticism of law enforcement. Nobody likes to see their work go to waste. In my experience, law enforcement personnel do not like situations where they respond to the same residences over and over to deal with the same people over and over only to see nothing ever come of it. It is not reasonable to expect law enforcement to devote time and resources towards a futile effort.

When successful prosecution rates are low and law enforcement personnel are not on board, it is bad for victims. When law enforcement is participating in less domestic violence training and are not devoting the time and resources necessary to support an evidence-based approach, the cases they submit will not be as strong. There will be less evidence other than the victim's statement. For the prosecutor, that means the difficult task of overcoming uncooperative victims and absent victims becomes even harder. Also, the problem bleeds over into domestic violence cases with cooperative victims because those cases will also not be as strong. Thus, successful prosecution rates fall even further. It is a downward cycle.

On the other hand, higher successful prosecution rates work to convince law enforcement to make domestic violence cases a priority. In my experience, law enforcement personnel are far more likely to attend domestic violence training and apply that training when their efforts lead to positive results.

When victims are compelled to appear, results will follow. Those results work to convince law enforcement personnel to get on board. Once they are, the cases they submit become stronger, and successful prosecution rates rise.

In my opinion, it is not possible to have effective evidence based domestic violence prosecution unless there is a firm no-drop policy where victims are compelled to appear. Compelling victims to appear leads to higher successful prosecution rates, less need for victims to testify, increased intervention in abusive relationships to reduce escalation, more engaged law enforcement, more encouragement for victims to report abuse, and more batterer accountability.

The alternative approach leads to much lower successful prosecution rates, more victims trapped further in abusive relationships, less intervention, greater likelihood of escalation, more witness tampering and intimidation, frustrated and less engaged law enforcement, discouragement for victims to report abuse, and less batterer accountability. The alternative approach is what makes monsters like Tommy Castro possible. During my time in Ada, I was part of an effective evidence-based approach to handling domestic violence. The foundation of this was compelling victims to appear. Without that pillar, the whole thing would have collapsed. That is way too high a price to pay just to protect victims from testifying. Compelling victims to appear, even if that means contempt actions or warrants, is hands down the better approach.

There are two additional points about compelling victims to appear that must be addressed. First, willingness to issue warrants reduces the need to do so. During my time in Ada, I was not shy about our policy. When the policy is to compel victims to appear and everyone knows it, then when victims ask if they must appear, they receive a consistent answer.

This is something advocates and counselors should be encouraged to discuss with victims who are receiving services. Defense attorneys will likely tell victims the same answer when they are asked. Also, this issue would sometimes come up when I was meeting with a victim. I would try to be diplomatic about it, but I would be straight-forward and honest that appearing in court was not voluntary. During my six years working in Ada, there were only three instances where a contempt action or warrant was necessary.

The second point is that compelling victims to appear requires serving them with their subpoenas. There is no way to compel a victim to appear if that victim was not properly served. The requirements for proper service may not be the same in every state.

During my time in Ada, subpoenas were personally served on the victim by a deputy sheriff. Service by mail, service by publication, or service to a third party, such as a person residing with the victim, was not proper service. Without proper service, there is no basis for any contempt action or warrant for an absent victim.

Batterers know that, and intimidation and tampering activities typically lead to victims trying to avoid service. Since an evidence-based approach requires victims to be present, and that requires proper service, it can be fairly stated that effective domestic violence prosecution often boils down to the struggle between the prosecutor and the batterer over getting the uncooperative victim served.

Thus, being an effective domestic violence prosecutor requires being successful in locating victims and getting them properly served. A discussion of the important role that partner agencies play in serving subpoenas can be found in

Chapter Five. During my time in Ada, it was my experience that uncooperative victims typically honored subpoenas once they were served.

As previously mentioned, the victim's presence provides leverage in plea negotiations, but calling domestic violence victims to the witness stand cannot be eliminated. There will always be some category three cases where the victim must testify. For these cases, there are steps that a prosecutor can take to mitigate the consequences victims face.

Similarly to how overcoming uncooperative victims begins with the initial law enforcement response, so should efforts to mitigate consequences for victims taking the stand.

In places where the LAP is used, the questions mostly require yes or no answers. If the victim answers yes to enough of the questions, then the victim "screens in." Whenever a victim screens in, it is mandatory to immediately call an advocacy center or the domestic violence hotline and connect the victim with an advocate or counselor.

In my experience, a large majority of victims screen in. The ensuing phone call serves as an ice breaker between the victim and a victim services provider. The goal is for that call to lead to the victim receiving additional services both while the case is pending, and after it has been resolved.

Based on conversations I have had with victim services providers, the likelihood that a victim will seek additional services depends in part on how well trained the officer is for conducting the LAP. When the LAP is conducted by a specially trained domestic violence officer who can discuss the real dangers of abusive relationships with the victim, the victim is more likely to receive services.

When the officer conducting the LAP does nothing more than ask the questions, check the boxes on the form, and then initiate the phone call, the victim is less likely to seek additional services. When a victim is receiving counseling or other services, it can help make the consequences of testifying easier to manage.[118] Thus, it is important for a prosecutor, or the District Attorney's Office, to work with law enforcement to ensure that there are specially trained domestic violence officers available.

The second step is to minimize witness intimidation. There are several ways to reduce this. For example, there should be a routine practice that disallows victims from visiting the defendant at the jail. Courthouse security personnel can also help by chaperoning inmates while they are at the courthouse to keep them isolated from the victim. Screening jail calls will also help. Whenever I had a victim recant, minimize, or in some other way become uncooperative, I immediately requested any jail calls between the defendant and either the victim or the defendant's family to see if there was any content that might support a Forfeiture by Wrongdoing or intimidation action.

Furthermore, judges may impose no-contact orders in domestic violence cases as a condition of bond or release. These orders were standard for domestic violence cases during my time in Ada, and we enforced them with bond revocation motions and contempt charges for defendants caught in violation.

To that end, we had a system for informing law enforcement when the orders were issued. Otherwise, if law enforcement encountered a violation of a no-contact order, they would not realize it. Finally, an active Coordinated

Community Response Team, which helps facilitate greater inter-agency communication and cooperation, can help bring to light intimidation efforts that are taking place outside of the criminal justice arena.

The policy of compelling victims to appear can also be a tool to help minimize witness intimidation. Compulsive appearance shifts the decision away from the victim and empowers them to use that fact as a shield against intimidation.

The victims can tell their batterers, their batterer's family, or anyone else, that it was not up to them to appear or not. Victims can also tell those people that they tried to avoid having to testify but it was not their choice.

Another step is to employ a consistent practice of keeping victims separated from public access when they are at the courthouse. Typically, this involves having the victim and anyone accompanying them arrive at the prosecutor's office first before being escorted to a private witness area in the courthouse. During my time in Ada, that was our practice. We would routinely communicate with victims and courthouse personnel to make the necessary arrangements. This practice protected victims from any contact or confrontation with the batter or anyone that might be present in the courthouse on the batterer's behalf, such as the batterer's friends or family.

Lastly, some of the consequences can be mitigated when the victim has people with her for support. In Ada, we routinely informed victims of their right to have support when they appeared. That included an advocate or counselor and any friends or family that they chose. We explained to victims that, when they appeared to testify, they could bring any friends or family that they wanted. Their friends and family could stay with them in the witness waiting area and be in the courtroom while the victim testified, provided they were not also potential witnesses. To further facilitate this, our victim/witness coordinator or an advocate would be on hand when the victim arrived to ensure that the victim would have at least one support person available.

Nearly all the concepts, approaches, and strategies discussed in this book were in place after I returned from the Portland conference in January of 2013. The results from 2013 are the first examples of what our evidence-based approach and firm no-drop policy were capable of once everything was up and running.

Also, all the agencies and people involved continued to learn and improve through practice and experience. Thus, the results from 2014 and 2015 provide even better examples. In 2013, our office received 102 domestic violence intakes from law enforcement.[119] Of those, 99 led to criminal charges. Just three were declined. Out of 99 cases filed, 84 were successfully prosecuted.[120] Our successful prosecution rate for 2013, factoring in declined files, was 82%. In 2014, our office received 118 domestic violence intakes. Of those, 117 led to criminal charges. Just one intake was declined. Out of 117 cases filed, 105 were successfully prosecuted. Our successful prosecution rate for 2014, factoring in the declined file, was 89%. In 2015, our office received 140 domestic violence intakes. Of those, 140 led to criminal charges. None were declined. Out of 140 cases filed, 117 were successfully prosecuted. Our successful prosecution rate for 2015 was 84%.

Of those statistics, the one I am most proud of is that we filed all 140 intakes we received in 2015. That statistic, more than any other, illustrates how fully engaged our law enforcement personnel were when responding to domestic violence calls.

These results, collectively, also illustrate the upward cycle. Higher successful prosecution rates encourage law enforcement to be fully engaged and devote the necessary time and resources for an effective evidence-based approach. That, in turn, results in stronger cases, which leads to fewer declined intakes, more category one cases, and more category two cases where the batterer elects to take a deal once the victim appears.

Cases with cooperative victims also benefit when law enforcement is fully engaged. These results also reflect a high level of intervention, especially in misdemeanor cases, which helps prevent escalation. Finally, results like these encourage victims to report incidents of abuse because victims can be confident that something will come of it.

That the number of intakes rose from 102 to 140 within two years illustrates how increased confidence in the system increases victims' willingness to report domestic violence far more than fear of having to testify deters victims' willingness to report domestic violence. Results like ours are far better for victims and for promoting victim safety than the alternative approach. I am extremely proud of these results, and we achieved these results because we had more victims on our side.

CHAPTER FIVE

Have the Village on Your Side

E ffective evidence-based domestic violence prosecution requires a group effort. Regardless of how experienced, knowledgeable, or well-trained the prosecutor is, success or failure will depend on the contributions from partner agencies such as law enforcement and victim services providers.

Partner agencies have a role to play at every step, from the initial report through resolving the case, and in post-conviction enforcement. In the introduction, I described this as a coalition of agencies, each with their own "front" in the fight against domestic violence. I also described each partner agency as being a spoke on a wagon wheel with the prosecutor serving as the "hub." This is because the prosecutor is the person who works directly with every other agency in the coalition.[121]

It Takes a Village

It is important for the prosecutor to have a healthy working relationship with partner agencies. It is also important for the partner agencies to work well with each other. This chapter focuses on inter-agency cooperation and the role partner agencies play in effectively combatting domestic violence.

Some of the roles partner agencies play have already been discussed—for example, the importance of law enforcement being on board and fully engaged. The role that the jail administrators play with regards to recorded jail calls has also been discussed, and the role that victim services providers play with regard to participating in victim meetings and supporting victims who must appear in court or testify has been discussed.

There are several other ways that partner agencies contribute. The first is assisting victims with picking up the pieces. When a domestic violence case is successfully prosecuted, there is often hardship for the victim. I have seen many cases where, afterward, the victim was left in need of financial assistance, assistance with housing, and need of counseling. The prosecutor's primary responsibility is to hold the batterers accountable. In my experience, the District Attorney's Office has little to offer with regard to helping the victim deal with the aftermath. That is where victim services providers come in.

To receive services, a victim must be connected with a services provider. There are several steps partner agencies can take to help connect victims to victim services providers. One step, as previously discussed, is an effective LAP conducted by law enforcement.

Another step is for victim services providers to regularly obtain police reports related to domestic violence situations. During my time in Ada, both of the local victim services providers routinely visited the Ada Police Department and the Sherriff's Office to obtain reports.

The information in those reports allowed the services providers to reach out to victims. If local law enforcement agencies and local victim services providers have a healthy working relationship, then this step will be more effective.

Another step towards connecting victims and services providers is public awareness and community outreach. Increasing these efforts are things that law enforcement and the district Attorney's Office can assist with, but the victim services providers are the standard bearers.

Community outreach and public awareness are important for several reasons. One is that domestic violence victims are more likely to know where they can go for services. Another reason is that a more informed public increases the likelihood a victim will be encouraged to seek help through a friend or family member.

When a victim is caught in an abusive relationship, there are often signs or hints. If her friends or family becomes aware of the abusive relationship, they are likely going to act to help that victim or report the abuse. The victim's friends or family must know what the signs or hints are, however. Otherwise, even if they see the signs, they will not realize it. Effective community awareness and public outreach efforts can increase the likelihood that they will recognize the hints or signs that their friend or family member has been caught in an abusive relationship.

When the public is better informed, then a victim's friends and family are more likely to understand how prevalent domestic violence is in our communities. During my time in Ada, there were several events held each year to foster community outreach and public awareness.

A public candlelight vigil was held in the courthouse plaza each October to honor victims of domestic violence homicide. We held the vigil in October since that is Domestic Violence Awareness Month. Additional public events were held that included family friendly activities, run/walk events, motorcycle rides, and so forth.

These events had information booths, and representatives from all the involved agencies were on hand to educate the community and raise awareness. Based on my experience, greater public awareness results in more victims receiving services and increased reporting of domestic abuse. Also, greater public awareness can lead to a more informed jury pool.

Another way that partner agencies contribute is with locating victims. As previously mentioned, locating victims to serve subpoenas is critical. Sometimes, victims do not want to be found or served. Overcoming their resistance to being located or served often requires extra time and resources. Thus, it is critical to have a healthy working relationship with the agency responsible for serving subpoenas. One way to maintain that connection is to meet them halfway. What I mean by that is providing them with good information regarding the victim's address or location and endeavor to provide sufficient time for the task.

During my time in Ada, it was my regular practice to have subpoenas issued and delivered to the Sherriff's Office at least a month before the court date. That practice gave the Sheriff's Office sufficient time to assign the subpoena to a deputy. Also, in the event the first effort was unsuccessful, there would also be sufficient time to try and track her down. In such instances, our office took on the challenge of finding the victim. Once the victim was located, or new and credible information about the victim's location was obtained, I would issue a new subpoena (if necessary) and ask the Sherriff's Office to try again to serve the victim. It was an effective joint practice because I met the extra effort I was asking of them with extra effort of my own. It was helpful that the Sheriff's Office could be confident that, once a subpoena was served, our office would enforce it instead of allowing victims to not appear.

Tracking down a victim when the first attempt to serve a subpoena is unsuccessful is another area where partner agencies contribute. During my time in Ada, there were several steps our office took to track down victims. One step was to enlist the aid of the case agent or lead investigator to help with the search. Also, we would communicate with other state agencies that might have helpful information to share.

Not every agency can share the information in their possession. We were limited to information sharing that was lawful and in compliance with regulations. Still, in some cases, reaching out to other state agencies resulted in better contact information. Also, we would expand our search beyond the victim. We would try to locate people, such as close friends or family, who might be willing to assist in locating the victim.

In cases where the batterer was out of jail, we would try to track him down because it was likely that he and the victim were together. If the batterer was in jail, then another option, depending on the jail's policies, was to review inmate mail logs. In my experience, batterers and their victims often write letters to each other. The source or destination of any mail the batterer sent or received might help us find his victim.

After a case is successfully prosecuted, there is still a role that partnership agencies play. Post-conviction enforcement is an important aspect of combatting domestic violence. As I mentioned in the previous chapter, successful prosecution of domestic violence cases includes the batterer being ordered into counseling, such as a batterer's intervention program, or BIP. [122] Once the court orders the batterer to complete such a program, partner agencies contribute by running the programs and helping with enforcing the court's order. During my time in Ada, the victim services providers conducted the BIPs. In doing so, they also reported any batterers that were not in compliance with the order to complete the program. Probation or community supervision agencies, such as the Department of Corrections or a private entity, also contribute to enforcing the order by making sure that their client attends the program.

The post-conviction enforcement role is important. The BIP is a significant part of intervention. As I discussed in the previous chapter, intervention is important to reduce escalation in abusive relationships. In my experience, batterers who complete a BIP are less likely to re-offend; however, that only matters if batterers are completing the program. If batterers are being ordered into a program but are not complying with the order, then there will not be any effective intervention or reduced escalation. Also, batterers are often reluctant to attend or complete the program because, in my experience, they often have a strong dislike for the program. If nobody is making sure they are complying with the order, then, in many cases, they will not do so.

Ensuring that batterers are complying with the order requires two things. First, there must be an effective system in place to keep track of every batterer ordered into a program. That way, you know who is complying and who is not.

Second, there must be an effective system in place for holding non-compliant batterers accountable. That requires a consequence for non-compliance. The consequence needs to be significant jail time. I say jail because, in my experience, most non-compliance situations were misdemeanor cases. That was because most cases were misdemeanors and felony batterers on probation were typically more compliant because they faced greater consequences for non-compliance.

While there were instances where a felony batterer was sentenced to prison for not completing the program, those instances were rare. In my experience, the only thing that batterers hate more than the classes is jail. To have high completion rates for the programs, the batterers must be aware that, if they try to skip out on the program, they will be caught and incarcerated.

During my time in Ada, we had an effective system for keeping track of all convicted offenders who were ordered into a program. The agencies conducting the programs were notified of all batterers ordered into their program. That way, they could report anyone who did not show up.

The agencies were mandated to report any batterer who stopped attending or failed to complete the program. Supervising agencies were also informed any time they had a client that was ordered into a program. During my time in Ada, misdemeanor cases were supervised by the District Attorney's Office. Other supervising agencies were involved with felony cases. That way, they could remind their client about it and communicate with the agency conducting the program about their client's compliance. Non-compliant batterers were reported to my office for further prosecution.

By working as a team, and by sharing the workload, we enforced every order without any batterers falling through the cracks. That would not have been possible without the partner agencies.

Post-conviction supervision is not exclusively about counseling or the BIP. Increasing intervention and reducing recidivism are important, but domestic violence cases do not exist in a vacuum. In some cases, the batterer may have more than one charge and more than one type of problem, such as addiction. Now, let me be clear. I am not stating, suggesting, or implying that substance abuse or intoxication is a root cause of domestic violence. It is not. The root causes of domestic violence derive from power and control. Batterers can still be addicts, however. I have prosecuted many cases where the batterer had a substance abuse problem with either alcohol, illegal drugs, or prescription medications. In such cases, it is in society's best interest to address the addiction along with the domestic abuse.

With regard to misdemeanor cases, the available options I had for addressing addiction or substance abuse were limited. Typically, the batterer would be ordered to complete a substance abuse assessment and follow any recommended treatment.

In felony cases, more options were available. One of them was the Drug Court program. Admittedly, I opposed allowing felony batterers into the Drug Court program during my first four years as a prosecutor even though they were potentially eligible.[123] During that time, I treated any felony domestic abuse case as a violent crime.[124] During my last two years there, I modified that policy and allowed certain felony batterers into the Drug Court program if there was a substance abuse issue.

These instances were limited to felony cases that would have been misdemeanor cases but for a prior domestic abuse case serving as a valid enhancer and did not include any domestic violence case involving great bodily injury, strangulation, or the use of any weapon.

This policy change was part of an agreement with the Drug Court program. Allowing felony batterers into that program was initially their idea. I agreed based on certain conditions. The conditions included that batterers allowed into the Drug Court program had to complete their BIP and their case had to constitute a valid enhancer in the event they re-offended. Successful completion of the Drug Court program could result in the case being dismissed and expunged from the defendant's record; however, that outcome was not mandatory. Because dismissal and expungement might prevent the case from being a valid enhancer, that option was not available for felony batterers. Also, their BIP had to be incorporated into their Drug Court treatment plan, meaning that failure to complete the BIP would result in termination from the Drug Court program. Those conditions were met, so we began sending some felony batterers to the Drug Court program, and another agency joined our village.

For a village consisting of so many different partner agencies, communication is essential. One effective way to facilitate good relations is to get people from the various agencies together in one place. For that, a Coordinated Community Response Team (CCRT) is helpful.

During most of my time in Ada, we had a CCRT that met monthly. The meetings provided opportunities for agencies to share concerns, address problems, and seek advice from other agencies. The meetings also helped create familiarity and put faces with names. In my experience, cooperation between partner agencies is better when the people involved know each other. Also, the meetings facilitated discussion about specific cases or problems involving more than one agency. For example, our CCRT meetings were instrumental in having law enforcement and local medical facilities on the same page with regards to collection, preservation, and handling of forensic evidence. The various partner agencies in Pontotoc County communicated well and cooperated well. Thus, I had the village on my side.

We're Not Setting a Precedent

Even with good communication and cooperation, it will not always be smooth sailing. A domestic violence prosecutor will undoubtedly encounter situations where conflicts arise between partnership agencies. In my experience, such conflicts were not due to personality clashes or situations where certain people just did not get along, but rather arose from situations where the goals and priorities of one agency conflicted with those of another.

Each of the partnership agencies in the "village" has its own role to play, its own goals and priorities, and its own perspective. While all the agencies, in a broad sense, want to support victims and hold batterers accountable, there will still be instances where conflicts must be managed. One case I prosecuted in 2015 created two such conflicts.[125]

For this to make sense, some backstory about that case is necessary. The defendant was on probation for ten years in two felony cases when he was arrested in a new domestic violence case. His probation cases were for First Degree Burglary (along with other charges) and Child Neglect. Both First Degree Burglary and Child Neglect are 85% crimes in Oklahoma.[126]

The defendant was charged with Domestic Assault and Battery Resulting in Great Bodily Harm due to the victim's injuries, which included multiple bone fractures. He and the victim were not only in an intimate partner relationship, but also had a child together. In addition to a new felony charge, the assault violated his probation in both previous cases. Also, the defendant had a prior misdemeanor domestic abuse conviction from a previous incident where he had assaulted this same victim. Under those circumstances, the defendant faced a potential eight and a half years in prison if he was found to have violated the terms and conditions of his probation.[127]

For an experienced domestic violence prosecutor, there is nothing unusual about prosecuting a case where the victim suffered serious injury at the hands of a batterer who was already on probation.

The victim was receiving services from one of the local victim services providers that was part of our village. This case, however, was unique due to a pair of additional circumstances.

First, while the case was still being prosecuted, the victim suffered additional serious injuries in an unrelated accident that left her hospitalized for an extended period. Second, the defendant was a combat veteran who had served

overseas in Iraq. He had also served together in the Oklahoma Army National Guard with Deputy Page, who was
with the Pontotoc County Sheriff's Office.

The victim's injuries from the accident had a direct effect
on the case due to her limited mobility while she was
hospitalized. When the court date arrived for the preliminary
and motion to revoke hearings, the victim was unavailable
to appear in person to testify.[128]

I asked for a continuance to allow the victim additional
time to recover from her injuries and become available since
her unavailability was due to no fault by the State. At that
time, the defendant had been in jail since the date of his
arrest. If a continuance was granted the defendant would
have to stay in jail waiting for the new hearing date. The
defense counsel objected to the State's request for a
continuance and requested a bond reduction.

Neither party was at fault for the victim's unavailability.
Also, the defendant had a valid objection about having to
spend additional time in jail waiting for his hearing. As a
result, a deal was struck regarding the defendant's bond. The
parties agreed to a limited recognizance bond for the
defendant with certain conditions.[129]

First, the defendant's release was solely for the purposes
of in-patient treatment through Veteran's Affairs for
substance abuse and post-traumatic stress disorder issues.[130]
The court's order was that the defendant be transported from
the jail directly to the Veteran's Affairs facility in Oklahoma
City for treatment. A representative from Veteran's Affairs
assisted with arranging transportation and placement. The
limited release would allow the defendant to receive treatment he legitimately needed instead of sitting in jail.

The second condition was that the defendant have no contact with the victim. As I mentioned in Chapter Four, it was standard practice in Pontotoc County for any domestic violence defendant released from jail to be under a no-contact order from the court. The bond and limited release agreement were entered on the record, and both the defense counsel and the judge emphasized the importance of the no-contact order. The defendant stated that he understood that he was to have no contact with the victim in any way or for any reason.

I devoted all of chapter one to the importance of having the knowledge on your side. Well, in this case, I came up short in that area. The Veteran's Affairs hospital in Oklahoma City where the defendant went for treatment was right across the street from the hospital where the victim was recovering from her accident. I was not aware of that at the time the deal was made. Had I known that the defendant and his victim would be in such proximity, I never would have entered that agreement. I would have, at the very least, demanded that the defendant go to some other facility. When I found out that the two hospitals were across the street from each other, it was too late to do anything about it. The damage was done.

This is the point where the defendant's connection to Deputy Page became significant. Although Deputy Page was not involved in the investigation or arrest, he was familiar with the case. He had reviewed the facts and knew the defendant because of their service together in the National Guard. He took it upon himself to approach me to discuss the case, which I was happy to do. He and I had several conversations about the case. During those conversations, he gave me a great deal of insight into the defendant's service background and PTSD issues. Ultimately, he asked me to consider a treatment-based resolution instead of incarcerating the defendant.

It is important to understand the significance of his request. Deputy Page was no rookie. He had served our community as a law enforcement officer for many years. He had served our country in the military and deployed overseas and was still on active duty in the reserves.

Supporting other veterans was a very important issue for him. At the time of his request, he was also aware of the defendant's violent history, the serious nature of the charges, and the zero-tolerance approach I took towards domestic violence. So, there is no question he was asking me for a dramatic departure from how I would typically handle a case like this. He was also a person that I knew to be of upstanding sincerity and integrity. So, with all of that in mind, for him to approach me and ask me for such leniency was a big deal. He knew how serious of a request it was, and I knew how important it was to him for him to make it. I took his request very seriously.

Deputy Page's request constitutes the first conflict that arose out of this case. Typically, when a law enforcement agent approaches me about a case where the defendant has a violent history and is facing violent charges, their preference is for a firm or severe sentence as opposed to leniency or a treatment-based resolution. Now, to be clear, Deputy Page did not approach me in his capacity as a deputy. He approached me on his own behalf. So, he did not make his request on behalf of the Sheriff's Office; however, he was still a deputy, which means he was still a part of one of the partnership agencies in our "village," and he was advocating for leniency in a situation where my office has always sought severity.

After I received his request, the victim's medical situation once again became a hurdle. My initial response to him was that I would only consider his request if I had the victim's blessing, and even then, I was not making any promises. The hurdle was that she was still in the ICU and not in any position for me to talk to her about it. So, any conversations with her had to wait.

Eventually, the victim was moved from the ICU to a regular hospital room and had improved to the point where I could talk to her about the case. The victim services providers kept me up to date on her situation. I was not the only one to receive word that she was out of the ICU. The defendant also received word about where she was and her situation. In fact, the victim learned of his whereabouts and called him to ask him to visit her in the hospital. He accepted her invitation and visited her hospital room more than once. Obviously, each visit was a violation of his bond conditions.

The service providers helping the victim were aware of the no-contact order. A victim's advocate was present for one of the defendant's visits. The advocate reported his visit to her agency. That evening, I received a call about it and became aware that he had violated his bond conditions. That was the basis for the second conflict that arose out of this case.

As the prosecutor, I was obligated to enforce that bond condition. I could not simply wave a magic wand, however, and have the defendant transported back to jail. There was a process that had to be followed. It also would not have worked for me to file an unsubstantiated motion claiming that the defendant violated the no-contact order. That would have been thrown out. I had to file a written motion to revoke the defendant's bond that was supported by a factual basis. For that I needed the people who saw the defendant with the victim and knew who he was, to submit signed and notarized affidavits saying so. Once I received those affidavits, I could submit my motion with some evidence to back it up.

I received those affidavits and filed my motion, but the issue did not end there. The judge cannot just grant my motion and issue a warrant for the defendant. The process does not work that way. The defendant has a right to challenge my motion and have a hearing in open court. The defense received a copy of my motion, and the hearing was scheduled expediently.

A hearing means witnesses and testimony. So, now the victim's advocates were in a difficult position. Their agency and my agency were suddenly in conflict. I needed the advocates to testify about seeing the defendant in the same room as the victim; however, their obligation was to support the victim. She invited the defendant over to visit and did not want him to get into any trouble for visiting her.

The advocates also have rather strict and important confidentiality requirements they are responsible for. On top of that, their agency can suffer if they develop a reputation for siding against the very victims they are supposed to be supporting.

What ultimately happened was that the conflict between my office and the victim services provider was worked out in such a way that the advocate could appear and testify. The hearing proceeded and one of the advocates testified about seeing the defendant visiting the victim. The defendant's recognizance bond was revoked, and he was remanded back into jail. The resolution of that conflict and the outcome of the hearing, however, only exacerbated the first conflict.

When it comes to choosing between an incarceration resolution and alternatives to incarceration, such as traditional probation or a treatment-based resolution, one factor is whether the defendant is likely to comply with court-imposed conditions. Avoiding incarceration was already a steep uphill climb for this defendant due to the violent nature of his past convictions and the new charge. Also, the defendant was instructed repeatedly by both the judge and his attorney to have no contact with the victim while he was on his limited release and in treatment. He did not comply. If there was a single pivotal consideration affecting whether I would agree to a treatment-based resolution or not, that was it.

This case was one of the more difficult cases I handled as a domestic violence prosecutor. In addition to my discussions with Deputy Page, I also discussed it with the Sheriff as well as my own boss, the District Attorney. I also gave it a great deal of thought. I had to decide what I was willing to offer or agree to. It was not a decision I took lightly. While I did discuss it with other people, it was my decision to make. I was not about to try and pass it off to someone else. So, I made a decision.

The defendant ended up accepting a negotiated plea agreement. The first part of the agreement involved his probation cases. His suspended sentence in each case was for ten years; however, there is no requirement that the full term be revoked. The law allows for a suspended sentence to be revoked in part, and so that is what I agreed to.

Four years of each of his ten-year sentences were revoked. Thus, he was ordered to serve those four years in prison, including the 85% requirement, with credit for time already served in jail dating back to his original arrest.[131]

The main reasons why I agreed to revoke four years instead of the full sentence were his military service, his legitimate mental health and treatment needs resulting from his service, and because Deputy Page, who is someone I respect and consider a friend, asked me to show some leniency.

With regards to the pending charge, the defendant was given another probation sentence to run consecutively to his prison sentence. Once he is released from prison, he will begin a new twelve-year suspended sentence. That probation sentence would include certain conditions including a requirement that he report back to Veteran's Affairs and comply with any and all treatment recommendations they gave him for PTSD, any other mental health issues, and for any substance abuse issues. He would also be required to complete a BIP. It was not an easy decision, but in the end, I believe I made the right choice.

The key to managing conflicts such as these is good communication and good listening. The worst-case scenario is for conflicts like these to result in hard feelings and rifts between different people or agencies within the village. Hard feelings or divisions over a case can affect it as well as future cases.

With regards to Deputy Page, he and I had several conversations while the case was being prosecuted. I made sure to keep him informed about any progress being made, any court dates, and so forth. When I found out that the defendant had violated the no contact order, Deputy Page was the first person I called.

When I ultimately reached a decision about a resolution to the case, the first person I shared that with was Deputy Page. He was upset at first. He felt strongly about a treatment-based resolution. After agreeing to involve him in the case, and after so many prior conversations, I was not about to tuck tail and avoid him just because there was going to be a disagreement. We discussed the case and my decision at length. Even if we did not see eye to eye, at least we each knew where the other was coming from and cleared the air. Thus, there were no lingering hard feelings that might have affected future cases or dealings.

With regard to the conflict between my office and the victim services provider, I used the same approach. The conversations started when it came time to arrange for the advocate to testify. They had legitimate reservations about testifying due to confidentiality obligations, as well as the public perception of their agency.

My options were to either compel the advocate to appear and testify or to try and work with them with the hope that they would ultimately agree to have the advocate testify voluntarily. Compelling the advocate to testify was not a good option. That approach would likely result in hard feelings and would damage the working relationship between our agencies. So, I opted for the second approach.

Communication had to be a two-way street. One of my goals was to listen to their concerns and show consideration for their concerns; however, I needed them to reciprocate.

To that end, I reached out to them to explain my situation. The starting point for the conversation was the common ground that both agencies wanted the defendant held accountable for violating the no-contact order. I explained that holding him accountable was not possible without testimony in open court by someone who had seen both the defendant and the victim in the hospital room. They understood my position and we agreed there was no other option.

This was the point where the importance of having a healthy relationship with partnership agencies became evident. The victim service provider understood that I was asking for a significant concession and accepted that I would not be asking if it was not necessary. Ultimately, we were able to work out the conflict and they chose to allow the advocate to testify voluntarily.

After the hearing, I met with them again to make sure we cleared the air. During that conversation, they made it clear that they were not going to set a precedent where advocates appear in court, and that this was an exception they were willing to make for a serious case. In the end that conflict was resolved with no hard feelings or lingering tension.

For the village to function, it must be as co-equals where everyone is willing to make some concessions and show some consideration for everyone else. That includes the prosecutor. If the prosecutor tries to boss everyone else around, then success will be elusive. In Pontotoc County, we avoided that approach in favor of a more communal approach, and this case illustrates how our approach paid dividends.

Sail the Seven Keys

Successful domestic violence prosecution starts with the initial law enforcement response. The local law enforcement agencies are the most important partner agencies. The approach to combatting domestic violence discussed in this book, and all the goals involved, such as overcoming uncooperative victims, increasing successful prosecution rates, increasing intervention, decreasing recidivism, and so forth, depend primarily on the work product provided by law enforcement.

Two things are necessary for prosecutors to receive the best possible work product from law enforcement. These are things that the prosecutor can influence.

First, law enforcement must be fully engaged and willing to devote the necessary time and resources to domestic violence cases.

Second, the law enforcement personnel working in the field must be trained to properly handle domestic violence cases. During the last few years of my time in Ada, our office influenced the second of these by providing training for law enforcement twice per year.

Each training event our office hosted involved four presenters. While the other three presenters changed from one event to the next, my training presentation was always included. My main focus was on initial law enforcement response. The core premise was that law enforcement should approach a domestic violence incident under the presumption that the victim will ultimately be uncooperative.

Operating under that presumption is important for two reasons. First, it means treating the initial response as their

155

only opportunity to collect evidence, and that any evidence left behind is lost forever. Second, it means placing an emphasis on collecting all other evidence aside from the victim's statement. Within that core premise, I detailed seven steps that law enforcement should take during a domestic violence response. I called them the seven keys to success in overcoming uncooperative victims.

The first key is to speak to everyone who was present or within hearing distance of the incident. This included participants in the altercation, witnesses, any other people in the residence or close by, neighbors who may have heard the altercation, and so forth. This is one area that requires law enforcement to devote more time to domestic violence responses. Even if there are multiple officers or deputies on the scene, it takes more time to interview more people. Thus, it is an area that will suffer when law enforcement is not fully engaged.

It is worth the extra time and effort. More descriptions of what happened paint a clearer picture. Also, third-party accounts can corroborate the victim's original version of events. In my experience, most domestic violence responses happen shortly after the incident. In such cases, there is typically little opportunity for people at the scene to collaborate or fabricate anything. Thus, whenever a third-party account supports the victim's account, it is crucial evidence. Also, third party accounts might include incriminating statements by the batterer. For example, in one case I prosecuted, a third party witness' statement included an exchange where the batterer told her that the victim fell on the stairs, to which she replied, "Y'all don't even have stairs."[132] Evidence of that nature is only useful if it is collected.

A third-party witness can also be helpful in the event of a bond hearing because that witness can testify in place of an uncooperative victim. In cases with uncooperative victims and batterer's unable to make bond, a bond hearing is typical. In such hearings, it is likely that the uncooperative victim will appear to testify to the reasons why she wants the bond reduced and the batterer released. It can be helpful for the judge or magistrate to also hear from a third-party witness to the assault before making a ruling.

Of course, not every domestic violence incident is reported immediately. I have seen many cases where the incident was not reported until a third party brought the victim in to make the report after the fact. In such cases, it is crucial for law enforcement to interview that third party. Typically, that person is a close friend or family member. Also, since that third party brought the victim in to make a report, then the victim must have told that third party what happened. Thus, it is important that law enforcement interview or take a written statement that includes everything the victim said about the incident.

The second key is to insist on specific details. This applies to all witnesses but is particularly important with regard to the victim. The more specific information law enforcement can obtain at the scene, then the harder it will be for the victim to later craft an alternative version of events. Obtaining more specific details serves to lock the victim into her original version. This key requires asking follow-up questions to vague or general statements. For example, if a victim tells law enforcement that "he hit me," then some more digging is necessary. A general statement like that should be followed by questions such as "Do you remember how he hit you?"; "Do you recall what he hit you with?"; "Can you point to where on your person he hit you?"; "Were you able to tell how many times he hit you?"; "Are you injured?"; "Do you know whether you tried to fight back?"; or "Can you point out where you were located when he hit you?"

This key also requires asking follow-up questions about anything that seems unclear, contradictory, or verifiable. A common example of something verifiable is when the batterer breaks the victim's phone. In this case, the phone needs to be found and examined to see if it is broken. Items like this are strong evidence.

The third key is to visit the scene of the altercation. Most domestic violence incidents happen inside a residence. Once law enforcement arrives at the scene, their initial contact with people is typically outside the residence or at the door. It is important for law enforcement to employ any available means, within reason and under the law, to gain access to the room where the altercation took place.

This requires either valid consent or another legal means, such as a valid search warrant. In some instances, there will be no consent, and it can take time to obtain a warrant. The delay can cause any subsequent search or access to be fruitless. In my experience, law enforcement typically receives valid consent if they make a reasonable request for access and can then visit the scene.

Once at the scene, law enforcement should look for signs of a struggle. Two or more adults fighting inside a room typically leaves signs such as broken or displaced furniture or fixtures, blood, loose hair, and so forth. Such evidence is important for several reasons. First, it is proof that there was an altercation that can be photographed and documented. Second, the signs of a struggle might corroborate details provided by the victim or other witnesses in their statements.

For example, in one case I prosecuted, the victim's statement included that the batterer grabbed a hat off her head and, in doing so, pulled out some of her hair.[133] During the initial response to that case, law enforcement gained access to the scene and found a hat on the floor with a lot of hair in it, which corroborated the victim's claim. Finally, such evidence can serve as the basis for additional questions. If there are signs of a struggle that have not been fully explained, then law enforcement should seek a detailed explanation and ask more questions.

The fourth key is to obtain and review written statements from the victim and witnesses while at the scene. The reason it is important to obtain the written statements at the scene is so that they can be reviewed before law enforcement leaves. For the victim's statement, this is crucial. This is another area that requires law enforcement to devote more time to domestic violence responses. Like with interviews, it takes more time to collect statements from more people at the scene, and it takes more time to read them.

Just like the first key is worth the extra effort, so is this one. One reason it is important for law enforcement to review written statements at the scene is to make sure that they match the verbal statements. If the victim said one thing and then wrote something different, then that is a problem. It is important for law enforcement to catch that before they leave so the problem can be addressed to figure out why

159

there is a discrepancy. Another reason it is important is when the written statement is either brief or overly general. The more general the statement is, the less valuable it is. If the victim's written statement is just two or three sentences or lacking in details, it is important for law enforcement to catch that before they leave so they can ask the victim to keep writing. Obviously, law enforcement cannot instruct the victim on what to write, but in such cases, the victim typically gives a much more detailed verbal statement than a brief written statement. Thus, law enforcement should simply ask her to write out the same things she told them verbally and do so honestly. If law enforcement clears the scene and finds out later that there is a problem with the victim's written statement, it is unlikely that there will ever be an opportunity to address it.

Another circumstance that I have encountered is where the victim gives a brief or general verbal statement to law enforcement, and then provides a long and detailed written statement. In my experience, this is rare. In cases where I have seen this happen, it was because the victim was afraid that other people at the scene, such as the batterer or people present that might be sympathetic to the batterer, might hear what she said. As a result, she said very little and wrote a lot. In such cases, law enforcement needs to read that statement to get the details they need about the incident. Otherwise, they will not be able to follow the second key.

Finally, obtaining a written statement from the victim at the scene is important because that may be law enforcement's sole opportunity to do so. I am opposed to the practice of leaving blank statement forms for the victim or witnesses to fill out and return. It is rare for those statement forms to ever get filled out or turned in. There are always exceptions. Victims with serious injuries that need medical attention cannot write a statement at the scene. Victims who are intoxicated or under the influence of controlled substances also cannot write a statement until they have a clear head. In these situations, there is no other choice besides trying to obtain a statement later; however, even with those exceptions in mind, domestic violence cases that have no written statement from the victim should be avoided when at all possible.

The fifth key is to take photos. Photograph anything that is relevant. That includes injuries, weapons, signs of a struggle, broken phones, or anything verifiable that was included in the victim's statement. In addition to their evidentiary value, photos are important because they are available immediately and allow the prosecutor to present them when the batterer makes his initial court appearance. Photos of the victim's injuries can strengthen a prosecutor's argument that the batterer is a danger to his victim. The court can consider the photos before deciding about the batterer's release or imposing a bond or security amount.

The sixth key is to verify phone numbers. Contacting the victim and other witnesses is important. That requires working phone numbers. Sometimes witnesses omit phone numbers from their statements. It is common for victims to write false numbers on their statements. Thus, while law enforcement personnel are at the scene, they should make a reasonable effort to verify that phone numbers are provided and that they are accurate. With regards to victims, this can also be important for obtaining jail call recordings since some jail phone systems can be searched by the number dialed.

The seventh key is to not be confrontational with victims. This key is the most important of the seven keys to success. The reason this key is important is that it often affects whether the other keys can be followed. It is important for law enforcement to understand that, when victims are uncooperative, it is due to fear and the effects of trauma. Victims rarely refuse to cooperate so they can make life difficult for law enforcement. Also, it is important to understand that any fears a victim has are valid and typically create hardships for her. Whatever she is afraid of will happen is likely going to happen. Thus, it is important for law enforcement not to be deterred or frustrated by uncooperative victims at the scene.

Being confrontational is about tone and demeanor. A confrontational interaction with a victim involves an authoritative posture, an aggressive or commanding tone, or a demeanor consistent with anger or frustration. I have watched many body camera videos from domestic violence responses. In my experience, a confrontational "hard eyes" approach will cause a victim to withdraw, resist, and shut down. That likely means less detailed answers, no access to the scene, no permission to take photographs, and so forth.

Alternatively, a conversational and empathetic "soft eyes" approach can have the opposite effect. It is important to note that an officer or deputy can still be persistent with a conversational approach. Persistence is fine. Information needs to be discovered. It is the tone and demeanor that matter. A conversational approach is far more likely to result in more detailed answers, access to the scene, permission to take photographs, and so forth.

I am aware of the burdens these keys place on law enforcement. Time is an issue and following them can be a tall order when there are a lot of calls to respond to. When I presented this material to law enforcement, I raised this issue. In doing so, I addressed the time demands with several points.

First, if the keys to success become regular practice, then they do not take as long. I have handled many cases where the responding officers did a good job following the keys and were on scene for less than twenty minutes. There are other cases, such as those involving more witnesses, that took longer.

Second, sharing the work between several people can lessen the burden.

Third, following the keys will produce results, so it is not wasted time or wasted effort.

Fourth, the more consistently law enforcement responders follow the keys at the scene, the less likely they must testify later.

Finally, I tell law enforcement that there will often be opposing needs and competing interests because circumstances will rarely be ideal. Thus, my hope is that they will make these keys to success a point of emphasis, manage situations the best that they can, and trust their judgment.

The principle behind the seven keys to success is to leave no stone unturned and to leave no evidence behind because law enforcement will likely only get one shot at it. Such a thorough approach is necessary to overcome uncooperative victims. When law enforcement is fully engaged and following the keys to success, that is the most important component of having the village on your side.

Let the Evidence be Your Guide

What if she is lying? While it is rare in my experience, false claims of abuse happen. This book describes and advocates for an aggressive approach toward combatting domestic violence. Thus, wrongful convictions are a danger. So, within a system focused on overcoming uncooperative victims and succeeding in court despite recanting victims, how do you prevent false accusations from leading to wrongful convictions?

That is an important question, and because my approach is about holding batterers accountable and protecting victims and not about notches on the prosecutor's belt, the same keys to success for overcoming uncooperative victims are the keys to success in identifying false claims of abuse.

Asking more questions, insisting on more details, and addressing any omissions or inconsistencies will reveal any cracks or holes in a false claim of abuse and protect against wrongful convictions.

NOTES

Chapter One

[1] Throughout this book, I cite statutes and the evidence codes. Like many states, the evidence codes in Oklahoma, Washington, and Idaho are based on the Federal Rules of Evidence and follow a similar numbering system. Criminal statutes vary significantly from state to state, however, requiring that the material presented in this book may have to be molded to fit statutes from other states.

[2] See Title 21 of the Oklahoma Statutes Sections 644 and 644.1.

[3] See Revised Code of Washington (RCW) 10.99.020(4), 10.99.020(7), and 10.99.020(8).

[4] See Title 18 of the Idaho Statutes Section 18-918.

[5] See Title 18 of the Idaho Statutes Section 18-923.

[6] See Title 21 of the Oklahoma Statutes Sections 644(I), 644(N), and 644(P).

[7] See RCW 9A.36.041(3)b), RCW 7.105.450(4) and (5), RCW 9A.46.020 (2)(b), and RCW 9A.46.110(5)(b).

[8] See Title 18 of the Idaho Statutes Section 18-918.

[9] See Title 18 of the Idaho Statutes Section 18-918.

[10] See Title 18 of the Idaho Statutes Section 18-923.

[11] The Power and Control Wheel was first developed by the Domestic Abuse Intervention Project in Duluth Minnesota in 1984.

[12] Enhancement statutes are those that allow a defendant's criminal history to affect the charges or potential punishment in a new case.

[13] The jury instruction for a specific charge specifies the elements of that charge, so it is very helpful to be familiar with the OUJI.

[14] This decision requires understanding each element of the crime charged to make sure that evidence supporting each element is present.

[15] Pontotoc County case number CF-2011-244

[16] Oklahoma law defines "strangulation" as any form of asphyxia; including, but not limited to, asphyxia characterized by closure of the blood vessels or air passages of the neck because of external pressure on the neck or the closure of the nostrils or mouth because of external pressure on the head. See Title 21 of the Oklahoma Statutes Section 644(J). The precise definition may vary in other states.

[17] Note that each state has its own definitions for proving strangulation or attempted strangulation.

[18] The actual amount of pressure necessary to cut off blood flow to the brain was included as part of the strangulation section of the Portland

conference. Also, according to the Institute on Strangulation Prevention, the required pressure to cut off blood flow through the Carotid Artery is 11 pounds per square inch and for the jugular vein 4 pounds per square inch.
[19] It is common for victims of strangulation to describe what happened using the word "choked" even though that term refers to an internal blockage of the trachea and not external pressure.
[20] Defendants who spent little or no time in jail obviously did not make many calls on the jail phone system.
[21] Cases and statutes relevant to forfeiture by wrongdoing include *Reynolds v. US.* (98 U.S. 158), *Giles v. California* (554 U.S. 353), *Davis v. Washington* (547 U.S. 833), Federal Rule of Evidence 104(A), Federal Rule of Evidence 804, and Title 12 of the Oklahoma Statutes Section 2804(B)(5).
[22] For the domestic abuse cases filed in Pontotoc County Oklahoma in 2013 and 2014 about 29% were filed as Domestic Assault and Battery in Presence of a Minor.
[23] The case on trial was Pontotoc County case number CM-2010-254.
[24] The case on trial was Pontotoc County case number CM-2010-724.
[25] I chose not to mention Idaho here because my domestic violence case load in Idaho consisted almost entirely of felony cases.
[26] Note that this is not always the case. In one case I prosecuted, the victim met with me while a third party was present. In a jail call recording between that victim and her batterer, she said that she viewed the third party as a potential witness, which made her more apprehensive. I have chosen to omit a case reference to protect the victim's identity.
[27] Oklahoma law requires that any person charged with certain domestic violence offenses complete Attorney General certified domestic violence counselling as a condition of probation. See Title 21 of the Oklahoma Statutes Section 644(G)(1) and (G)(2).
[28] This is a reference to concepts such as the cycle of violence, power, control, isolation, and dependence. While I have a reasonably solid grasp of the dynamics of abusive relationships, I am neither a victim advocate nor a domestic violence expert, and so I have chosen not to explore those concepts in this book.
[29] I have chosen to omit a case reference to protect the victim's identity.

Chapter 2

[30] These laws also place guidelines on what constitutes a prior conviction and whether the prior conviction is too old to be used as to enhance a new charge. See for example Title 21 of the Oklahoma

Statutes Sections 644(N) and 644(P), Title 9A of the Revised Code of Washington Section 9A.36.041, and Title 18 of the Idaho Statutes Section 18-918.

[31] See Title 21 of the Oklahoma Statutes Sections 644(C), 644(E), 644(G), and 644(J).

[32] See for example Title 21 of the Oklahoma Statutes Sections 644(C), 644(E), and 644(G), Title 9A of the Revised Code of Washington Section 9A.36.041, and Title 18 of the Idaho Statutes Section 18-918.

[33] I have intentionally omitted reference to the defendant's name, the county where the cases were filed, or what years the cases were filed. Making my point contains no need for me to expose the people who prosecuted those cases in the process, and it is not my intent to criticize or judge their decisions.

[34] See for example Title 21 of the Oklahoma Statutes Sections 644(I), Title 9A of the Revised Code of Washington Section 9A.36.041, and Title 18 of the Idaho Statutes Section 18-918.

[35] In order to convict a person of an enhanced offense the State has the burden to prove that the applicable prior conviction exists. Court records for the prior conviction are necessary to do so.

[36] See, for example, Oklahoma Court of Criminal Appeals case *Fairchild v. State* (998 P.2d 611).

[37] Ibid.

[38] See Title 21 of the Oklahoma Statutes Sections 644(C), 644(E), 644(F), and 644(G).

[39] See Title 18 of the Idaho Statutes Sections 18-903(a) and 18-918.

[40] See Title 18 of the Idaho Statutes Section 18-923.

[41] Minimizing refers to instances where a domestic violence victim does not recant her original claim but instead tries to justify or excuse what happened to some degree or in some other way tries to make the abusive conduct appear less serious.

[42] Typically, these defense arguments are based on *Brill v. Gurich* (965 P.2d 404) in Oklahoma, Superior Court Criminal rule 3.2 in Washington, and Criminal Rule 46 in Idaho.

[43] See Title 22 of the Oklahoma Statutes Section 1105(B).

[44] See Washington Superior Court Criminal Rule 3.2(2)(b).

[45] See Idaho Criminal Rule 46(c).

[46] See Title 12 of the Oklahoma Statutes Section 2804(B)(5), Washington Rule of Evidence 804(b)(6), and Idaho Rule of Evidence 804(b)(5).

[47] See *Daubert v. Merrell Dow Pharmaceuticals* (509 U.S. 579) and its progeny.

[48] See *Taylor v. State* (889 P.2d 319).

[49] See Title 22 of the Oklahoma Statutes Section 40.7.

---

⁵⁰ For Washington, see *State v. Ciskie* 110 Wash.2d 263 (1988) and *State v. Case* 466 P.3d 799 (2020). For Idaho, see *State v. Guel*, (2012 WL 9495945 unpublished opinion) and *State v. Ibarra*, (2014 WL 4345833 unpublished opinion).
⁵¹ See Title 22 of the Oklahoma Statutes Sections 991a(A)(1) and 991a(E).
⁵² See Title 22 of the Oklahoma Statutes Sections 991b(A).
⁵³ Ibid.
⁵⁴ See Title 12 of the Oklahoma Statutes Section 2103(B)(2).
⁵⁵ See Title 22 of the Oklahoma Statutes Sections 991b(B)(2)
⁵⁶ See Idaho Rule of Evidence 101(e)(3).
⁵⁷ Pontotoc County case number CF-2012-578.
⁵⁸ While Oklahoma has a specific statute for Domestic Abuse Against a Pregnant Woman with Knowledge of the Pregnancy under Title 21 of the Oklahoma Statutes Section 644(E), that section is a misdemeanor first offense whereas the Great Bodily Injury charge under Section 644(F) is a felony first offense.
⁵⁹ Pontotoc County case number CF-2014-75.
⁶⁰ Oklahoma law allows for an accelerated timeframe for the hearing. See Title 22 of the Oklahoma Statutes Sections 991b(A).
⁶¹ See Title 21 of the Oklahoma Statutes Section 643.
⁶² The Committee Comments for the jury instruction regarding the burden of proof applicable to a self-defense claim include that self-defense can be raised as an issue if sufficient evidence is brought by the prosecution.
⁶³ See *Perez v. State* (798 P.2d 639).
⁶⁴ There is no definitive rule for what constitutes sufficient evidence to raise self-defense; however, see *West v. State* (798 P.2d 1083) and *Lumpkin v. State* (683 P.2d 985) as examples where there was insufficient evidence.
⁶⁵ See *West v. State* (798 P.2d 1083).
⁶⁶ Out of professional courtesy to the prosecutor trying the case, I have chosen not to divulge when or where this trial took place.
⁶⁷ Note that I am not discussing domestic violence homicide cases here. The rules of evidence regarding the victim's character are different in homicide cases where the defendant seeks to raise self-defense. See *Harris v. State* (400 P.2d 64).
⁶⁸ See Title 12 of the Oklahoma Statutes Section 2404.
⁶⁹ See Title 12 of the Oklahoma Statutes Section 2404(B).
⁷⁰ See *State v. Alexander*, 52 Wash App 897 (1988), and *State v. Custodio*, 136 Idaho 197 (2001).
⁷¹ In Oklahoma proposed legislation goes to the District Attorney's Council. For Washington and Idaho, a prosecutor may find success

working through the Washington Association of Prosecuting Attorneys (WAPA) or the Idaho Prosecuting Attorneys Association (IPAA).
[72] See Title 21 of the Oklahoma Statutes Section 644.1
[73] Ibid.
[74] The definition of a prior pattern of physical abuse was broadened again by subsequent legislation effective November 1, 2016.
[75] Pontotoc County case numbers CF-2015-290 and CF-2015-500

Chapter Three

[76] See *Crawford v. Washington* (541 U.S. 36) and *Hammon v. Indiana* (Decided with *Davis v. Washington* 547 U.S. 813).
[77] See Title 12 of the Oklahoma Statutes Section 2403.
[78] See Title 12 of the Oklahoma Statutes Section 2801.
[79] See Title 12 of the Oklahoma Statutes Sections 2803(1), 2803(2), and 2803(3).
[80] See Title 12 of the Oklahoma Statutes Section 2803(6) and 2803(8).
[81] See *Crawford v. Washington* (541 U.S. 36).
[82] See *Davis v. Washington* (547 U.S. 813).
[83] See *Hunt v. State* (218 P.3d 516).
[84] See Title 21 of the Oklahoma Statutes Section 1211.1.
[85] See Title 21 of the Oklahoma Statutes Section 455.
[86] See *Hammon v. Indiana* (Decided with *Davis v. Washington* 547 U.S. 813).
[87] See *People v. Byrd* (855 N.Y.S.2d 505).
[88] This does not include privileged communications between attorneys and clients.
[89] See, for example, *United States v. Hammond* (286 F.3d 189), *United States v. Footman* (215 F.3d 145), *State v. Riley* (704 N.W.2d 635), *State v. Christensen* (737 N.W.2d 38), *State v. Modica* (186 P.3d 1062), and *State v. Favors* (43 So.3d 253).
[90] An offer of proof is an explanation to the court why a piece of evidence is relevant or admissible.
[91] See Title 12 of the Oklahoma Statutes Section 2801.
[92] See Title 12 of the Oklahoma Statutes Section 2803(6) and 2803(8).
[93] See Title 12 of the Oklahoma Statutes Sections 2803(8)(a) through 2803(8)(e).
[94] See Title 12 of the Oklahoma Statutes Section 2801(B)(2)(a).
[95] See Title 12 of the Oklahoma Statutes Section 2803(1) and 2803(2).
[96] See Title 12 of the Oklahoma Statutes Section 2504.
[97] See Title 12 of the Oklahoma Statutes Section 2504(D)(1).
[98] See Title 12 of the Oklahoma Statutes Section 2403.
[99] See *Miranda v. Arizona* (384 U.S. 436)

[100] I have chosen to omit a case reference to protect the victim's identity.

[101] A preliminary hearing is an evidentiary hearing where the State must show that there is probable cause that a crime has been committed and probable cause that the defendant committed the crime.

[102] Yes, he really said that.

[103] See Title 12 of the Oklahoma Statutes Section 2803(2).

[104] See Title 12 of the Oklahoma Statutes Section 2803(1).

[105] See Title 12 of the Oklahoma Statutes Section 2801(B)(2)(a).

[106] See Title 12 of the Oklahoma Statutes Section 2403.

[107] Pontotoc County case numbers CM-2015-219 and CF-2012-425.

[108] Pontotoc County case number CF-2013-388.

[109] See *Fernandez v. California* (571 U.S. ___).

[110] See Title 21 of the Oklahoma Statutes Section 142A-3(D).

[111] See Title 12 of the Oklahoma Statutes Section 2404(B).

[112] Ibid.

[113] I have again chosen to omit a case reference to protect the victim's identity. This video is from the same case referred to in the section titled *"The Apple Doesn't Fall"* near the end of Chapter One.

Chapter Four

[114] See item 37 of the FY 2016 Standard Special Conditions for Grants, which can be found at https://www.justice.gov/ovw/grantees. During my time in Ada, our office did not receive OVW grant funds. Thus, I was not subject to that condition. Also, I am opposed to that condition and, in my view, it should be removed.

[115] When evaluating successful prosecution rates, it is necessary to include declined cases. In the absence of a no-drop policy, it is possible to maintain higher successful prosecution rates for cases that are filed by declining to file intakes that are unlikely to be successful. Focusing exclusively on successful prosecution rates for cases filed paints a false picture. The more accurate approach is to determine the successful prosecution rates of domestic abuse cases submitted by law enforcement.

[116] My experiences have made me acutely aware of the progressive nature of abusive relationships. While I have not cited specific sources, there are many sources available that discuss this idea in detail. I encourage anyone who is so inclined to seek out those sources; however, further discussion or analysis of the progressive nature of abusive relationships is beyond the scope of this book.

[117] Incidents of domestic abuse involving the use of weapons, serious injuries, or strangulation are typically felonies even on the first offense.

[118] Note that victim services providers maintain a high degree of confidentiality. Other than victims who appeared in court with an advocate or counselor, I was typically unaware of which victims were receiving services and which were not. Thus, I have no means to know whether receiving services increases the likelihood of cooperation.
[119] The intake numbers for 2013, 2014, and 2015 do not include juvenile matters, sexual assault cases, or rape cases. The numbers include cases against adult defendants falling under any of the domestic violence offenses found under Title 21 of the Oklahoma Statutes Sections 644 and 644.1.
[120] Successful prosecution rates for 2013 and 2014 are as of July 2016. Successful prosecution rates for 2015 are as of May 2018.

Chapter Five

[121] Note that, because I worked in a low population jurisdiction, I was essentially a one-man domestic violence unit. In larger population areas, the activities discussed in this chapter are obviously more of a group effort.
[122] In Oklahoma, the BIP is a 52 week program involving weekly classes and either monthly or bi-monthly court appearances, and is regulated by the Attorney General's Office. See Title 21 of the Oklahoma Statutes Section 644(G)(2).
[123] In Oklahoma, a defendant could not enter the Drug Court program without approval from the District Attorney's Office. See Title 22 of the Oklahoma Statutes Sections 471.1 and 471.2.
[124] Note that none of the domestic violence offenses found under Title 21 of the Oklahoma Statutes Sections 644 and 644.1 are on the statutory list of violent offenses. See title 57 of the Oklahoma Statutes Section 571.
[125] This "case" involved three cases for a single defendant. Pontotoc County case numbers CF-2015-424, CF-2015-2, and CF-2009-353. The latter two were probation violation cases.
[126] The term "85% crime" refers to specific crimes that carry minimum service requirements for any term of incarceration. See Title 21 of the Oklahoma Statutes Section 13.1 subsections 12 and 14.
[127] Note that, in Oklahoma, the burden of proof for probation violations is preponderance of the evidence, and not the beyond reasonable doubt standard required in a criminal trial.
[128] When a defendant is facing new charges and probation violations it is common for the hearing on the probation violations and the preliminary hearing for the new charges to be a joint hearing since those hearings involve the same evidence.

[129] A recognizance bond means that the defendant is released from the jail on his promise to reappear without the defendant posting any monetary guarantee. Recognizance bonds can carry specific conditions that the defendant must comply with or risk having the bond revoked, which would result in the defendant being remanded back into jail or having a warrant issued for his arrest.

[130] It was understood and agreed upon by all parties that the defendant was dealing with PTSD because of his combat experiences.

[131] It was standard practice in Pontotoc County for an agreed plea deal involving incarceration to include giving the defendant credit for any time the defendant served in jail prior to entering a plea.

[132] Pontotoc County case number CF-2014-528

[133] Pontotoc County case numbers CF-2010-481 and CM-2010-1263.

www.ingramcontent.com/pod-product-compliance
Lightning Source LLC
Chambersburg PA
CBHW041933260326
41914CB00010B/1279